shine

shine

Discover a brighter you

LORRAINE KELLY

CENTURY

To my daughter Rosie,
who shines so very brightly and
makes the world a better place.

INTRODUCTION

With 35 years of crack-of-dawn starts behind me, I'm often asked how I manage to stay so energetic, day in, day out. At 60, I'm finally at a point in my life where I feel confident, happy and fulfilled, and I think that's what people are really responding to. That's not to say that I don't have my bad days. We all have such hectic schedules, time can run away with us. Whether it's work, housekeeping, looking after family, volunteering, caring for pets – the demands on our time are never-ending.

Just being human requires an incredible amount of effort and work. Days go past in a blur and, if you're not careful, the years run away from you and you end up thinking, 'Where has my life gone?'

Worse still, mental health is at an all-time low. I've had my own experience with this; the menopause triggered anxiety within me, which was scary, but with plenty of help I picked myself up and began to look forward to life again, and that's what I keep doing every day. I feel incredibly lucky not to have suffered from clinical depression, but I've seen others go to such dark places. We still have a way to go in tackling mental health, but we are now living in a world that's finally starting to take this condition seriously, and there is an increasing amount of help out there for those who are suffering.

You could write entire books on some of the subjects that I'll be covering in these pages, but I'm just going to pick out the highlights as I see them.

I'm not a doctor or a therapist, and I can't pretend to know everything, but I've certainly got experience and opinions.

You'll hear from some great experts I've worked with in the coming pages, but I can't overstate how important it is to speak to a professional and get medical and psychological advice for your own personal issues if you need to.

Remember that it's never too late to take stock and get what you really want from life. Every day that passes I understand myself a little better. My experiences, good and bad, have taught me that I need to seize the day. We only have one life. I want every day to feel bright and new, and I want to help other people make their lives shine too.

Sadly, I'm not a fairy godmother and don't have a magic wand that I can wave to make everything better in the world, but I've been lucky enough to meet some incredible people, in both my everyday and work life. I wanted to write this book so I could pass on some of the wisdom I've gained.

* * *

I am who I am because of my experiences. I certainly wasn't handed anything on a plate when I was growing up, and what I've achieved has been through my own hard work and tenacity. I didn't have anyone to help me get my foot in the door when I wanted to become a journalist, but I did have a strong sense of right and wrong, a curiosity about the world and the desire to challenge myself and be the best I could be.

I look back at my childhood with great affection. My mum, Anne McMahon, was only 16 and working in a record shop in Glasgow when she met my dad, John Kelly. He worked as an apprentice TV engineer in the same company (I always joke that my dad was in television). They were just kids and had no savings or material possessions. When Mum discovered that she was pregnant, she was just 17, and they decided to get married.

My mum had seven brothers and sisters. My grandmother wasn't up to looking after them all so my mum and her sisters – Helen, Josephine and Patsy – were sent to be brought up in a convent. The sisters were very close, but the relationship with their mother was fractious.

My grandmother was a most formidable woman and insisted that my mum went down south to have her baby and then give it up for adoption. My 17-year-old dad was having none of it, so he built up his courage and went to face the wrath of Granny Mac. I feel so proud thinking of my teenage dad standing up to his future mother-in-law and telling her: 'We're getting married and we're keeping the baby.'

There was no room for negotiation and my granny always had respect for my dad after that. My parents got married a few months later, in July 1959, and they have just celebrated 60 years of marriage. I came along that November, and for years I thought I was some kind of miracle child because I was 'four months premature'!

When I was born, my parents moved into a 'single-end' (a one-room, ground-floor flat) in the Gorbals, in the East End of Glasgow, which was once considered the poorest, roughest and most deprived area in Europe. We had no hot water, an outside toilet, and there was just a recess in the wall for the bed. When I was about three we moved into a tenement flat in Bridgeton, also in the East End of Glasgow. There, we had the luxury of an inside toilet and a dodgy water heater that was so unreliable Mum had to boil kettles for cooking and washing.

Although we didn't have a lot of money, I had a really happy childhood. I had parents who loved me and I didn't ever feel as if I wanted for anything. In fact, I felt very lucky compared to a lot of my friends, because I was so well looked after and I always knew how much my parents cared about me.

Our house was full of books, magazines and newspapers, and my parents had already taught me to read and write by the time I went to primary school, aged four and a half. My mum and dad weren't pushy, but they encouraged my younger brother, Graham, and me to read books – one of the greatest gifts I think any parent can give their child.

That love of reading has stayed with me to this day. Reading opens up new worlds; you can lose yourself in a good book and learn so much without it ever feeling like a chore. I'm sure those early years gave me my thirst for knowledge, because my parents inspired me so much. I got my fascination with astronomy from my dad – I must have been one of very few five-year-olds in the East End with a telescope!

I firmly believe our upbringing and early experiences have such a huge impact on our later life. Everything that I have been through – from being bullied at school, to loneliness, to becoming a mum – has made me who I am today, and I'm grateful for all those experiences, no matter how tough they were.

* * *

We all have the potential to shine; not just for other people, but for ourselves. We can't truly make other people happy until we've found our own happiness and contentment, and that feeling of quiet calm is what we're all searching for.

Whether it's parenting tips from my mum, a pearl of wisdom from one of my best friends or beauty tips from a Hollywood A-lister, everyone has got something to teach us. I've been like a sponge over the years, soaking up all this knowledge, and now I want to pass on the highlights to you. I want this book to be a bit like a giant hug and a comforting handhold for when you're feeling low.

I've split the book into three sections: Spark, Glow and Dazzle. Spark is a sort of first-aid kit for the glum days – my advice on how to get your mind in the right place. Glow is about self-care, ageing, style and beauty. Then the final section, Dazzle, looks at how you can take all of this newfound energy and apply it to your big-picture goals – whether that's starting a new project, making changes within your own world, or making a difference to your community.

Whether you want to discover the real you, feel more confident or give your life a bit of a general kick up the bum, you'll find tips galore to help you on your way.

I'm grateful to every single moment of the last 60 years – from my best to my worst – as they've all taught me something and helped me to shine. So come on, let's really try to make every day as fabulous as possible!

Love,

Lorraine xx

SPARK

Sometimes when you're feeling low it's hard to know where to begin with improving your life, and this can feel totally overwhelming. None of us expect to be happy all the time. We all know that, sadly, we'll all experience grief or loss in some form.

In some ways, it's harder when you can't put your finger on why you are feeling low. If you go through a break-up, for example, then as awful as you feel, you know that you need to focus on getting over your ex to feel better. It's an agonising process, and some days you'll feel like you'll be hurt forever, but at least you know what the source of your pain is.

This section is for all the people out there who feel like they're not quite at their best. If you feel like the days are passing by in a blur or that you could be that little bit happier, but you're not sure what to do about it, the first thing to do is look inwards, so this section is about maintaining a healthy mind. I think confidence, positivity, gratitude and assertiveness equip you to make the best decisions for yourself. I hope what you read in this section will help you to rediscover your spark and help you to be the best possible version of yourself.

HEALTHY THINKING

Everything starts with a healthy mind. You can own a wardrobe full of fancy frocks but you won't feel good in them unless your head is in the right place. A healthy mind equals a happy life, which is why it's so important to prioritise our mental health over everything else.

CONTENTMENT IS THE NEW HAPPY

We all have peak moments in our life, times when we are genuinely, truly happy and feel on top of the world, and we should cling on to those with both hands. Having my daughter Rosie was amazing, as was meeting and interviewing Leonard Nimoy who played my hero Mr Spock in *Star Trek*, going to Antarctica, standing next to Sir Ernest Shackleton's grave in South Georgia and toasting him with whisky, and getting an OBE from the Queen. These extraordinary experiences are the real highlights of my life, and these memories will stay with me for ever.

However, in between those snatched, beautiful experiences, life goes on. We can't sustain that level of joy where you feel like you're dancing on top of a rainbow. And that's where contentment comes in. Contentment is so underrated; we're all chasing the big moments that we'll capture in a picture to post on social media, but it's the day-to-day things that we really need to appreciate. It's those little bits of magic that add up to gratitude and fulfilment.

For me, contentment can be weeding the garden. You begin with a horrible and messy space, then later you walk away from a little haven that you've created yourself, and that feels great. I will bask in that good feeling for days and smile every time I look at my neat and tidy garden.

The best moments are often small things you take for granted, like your morning coffee or a quick phone call to your other half. You don't have to go far from home to take time out and appreciate incredible things. It could just be going to the park and looking at flowers and trees. I know that sounds airy fairy, but it's true.

I hold a little bank of memories to reflect on. If I'm feeling a bit low I'll take myself back to the time when Rosie and I drove along singing 'No Scrubs' by TLC in the car at the top of our voices. That instantly perks me up. Even thinking about the last thing that made you happy can start to change your mindset. Whatever gives you that little lift is brilliant.

It's too easy to dismiss the things that make our heart sing, because we often just take them for granted. We tend to notice the negative things but we don't appreciate how much we enjoy shopping for a card or present for someone we love, or being able to sit down and have dinner with our kids.

I said to a friend the other day, 'What little things make you happy throughout the day?' She replied, 'I don't think I have any. Sometimes my day is quite boring.' I asked her to really think about what gives her a little lift, maybe even without her realising, and within a few minutes she'd come up with a list:

- *Looking up at my garden and watching the birds come and go.*

- *Opening my wardrobe and having a choice of lovely clothes to wear.*

- *When my best mate phones me and we say 'good moaning' to each other because we've always got some silly gripe we'll laugh about together.*

- *My living-room rug, because I brought it back from one of my favourite holidays.*

- *My new kettle, because it's bright red and it makes me smile when I make a cup of tea.*

- *The catch-up chat my husband and I have every night when he gets in from work.*

- *A gin and tonic on a Friday night.*

Once she started she found it hard to stop. There were loads of small, wonderful things in her everyday life that make her that bit more sparkly on a daily basis, but she'd stopped noticing them.

I've never kept a gratitude journal – although I know a lot of people do, and they find it beneficial – but I do tot up my moments of gratitude in my head every day. Lots of parents nowadays make a habit of asking their kids what the favourite part of their day was, to try to encourage a positive mindset, but we should all get in the habit of doing that every night before we go to sleep.

The women who have inspired me in my life, like my mum or my teachers, taught me to be thankful for things every day. But they never sat me down and said, 'We're going to be inspirational and tell you how to live your life now'; they led by example and, above all, by being kind. They always told me that you get back what you put out and I do believe that. It's certainly not about being a goodie-two-shoes; it's just about being decent. If you are a good person, that goodness will come right back to you.

EXERCISE

What lovely things have you stopped noticing in your everyday life? As you go about your day, make a list of all the things you've started to take for granted – even if it's just the bus being on time or catching up on *Corrie*.

Anything that makes you feel better about yourself, and about the world in general, is valid. It doesn't need to be something huge, sometimes it can just be reading your favourite book or lighting a scented candle.

Things that went right today   Date: _____

_____

_____

_____

_____

_____

_____

_____

_____

NOT ALL ILLNESSES CAN BE SEEN

Our mental health is just as important as our physical health, but because emotional issues are often invisible, they're not always given the right level of attention.

I'm glad that as a country we've become so much better at talking generally about mental health, but we still need more resources to help people who are suffering, as there just aren't enough out there. As well as proper infrastructure, we have to create an environment for people in which they can admit they're struggling and don't feel ashamed to reach out. People should never have to worry that others will judge them or that they'll get sacked from their jobs or not considered for a promotion if they are open and honest about how they are feeling. Mental illnesses cannot have that stigma anymore. No one should have to just get on with it and cope with whatever life throws at them because they don't know how to ask for help.

Growing up, it was ingrained in me that you soldier on no matter what. If my brother and I were ill as kids, we didn't get a day off school unless we couldn't physically walk. My mum always taught me that you had a responsibility to get on with things and you couldn't let people down.

This is a great attitude to have in lots of ways, but not if you're truly struggling. It's one thing to crack on if you have a cold, but when it comes to mental health problems it's very different, as the smallest bumps in the road can feel like mountains. I get very upset when people tell others to 'man up' or 'pull themselves together'; that's not how it works, and it's a very old-fashioned view. If you could, of course you would, and it's the most unhelpful thing that anybody can say to you. If you have been brave enough to admit that you're not coping, I applaud you. Seek generous, kind people who will listen to you with compassion – they are out there, I promise.

REACH OUT

As I've mentioned, the menopause triggered anxiety for me. I would wake up in the early hours and go over and over things in my head – daft things that didn't really matter but felt massive when I was lying in a pitch-black room in a state of panic.

I was deeply unhappy and I felt that I wasn't in control. I could be toddling along quite nicely one day and then one small thing would happen that would throw me off balance. Someone would only need to say something the wrong way and that's all it would take to make me fall apart. I have always been a positive and resilient person, but I felt like I wasn't coping and I wasn't enjoying life. It was like all the joy had been sucked out of me.

I also felt constantly knackered. At first I put my exhaustion down to my job and not getting enough sleep, but I've been getting up early for over 35 years and had never felt that way before. I couldn't get excited about anything, even at occasions that should have been full of joy. At one of Rosie's birthday parties, I plastered on a smile and sleep-walked through it.

I always looked forward to Rosie's parties, but I didn't feel excited in the days beforehand, and I could barely remember it afterwards.

I became obsessed with insignificant concerns, and life just started to feel a little bit too much. Even if I just had friends coming over for the evening I would find myself getting into a state. I don't go to many events anyway, but I turned down every single invitation so that I didn't have to see people. I couldn't think of anything worse than going to a premiere or a work function. I was worried I'd look awful and knew I wouldn't be able to cope if I was torn apart in the press.

At other times I would agree to see pals and then cancel on the day because I couldn't face it. I even cancelled lunches with people I love because I just couldn't cope, which was so unlike me. I thought it was to do with getting older and that maybe I was becoming boring and unsociable, but now I know that was not the case.

Steve suggested that we went away, in case I just needed a break, but I couldn't leave my feelings behind. We went to Córdoba in Spain. It was a beautiful sunny weekend, but I had no energy or interest in what was going on around me. All of my usual enthusiasm had been drained from my body. I was, in a word, joyless.

During that time, my to-do list would loom over me like a giant black cloud, and I could barely stand to look at it. It wasn't as if it was filled with big things, either, they were just normal everyday chores that everyone gets on with without a second

thought, like sending an email or going food shopping.

Normally I would breeze through stuff like that, but I felt constantly panicked. I was so worried I would forget things I started to write to-do lists of to-do lists. I even had to write down things like 'research this guest', or 'get changed after the show', as if I was going to forget.

The rational part of my brain knew everything was OK but the irrational part kept trying to take over, and I couldn't control it. I knew I was getting anxious about things that didn't matter, but I couldn't get a handle on it.

I've always said there's no point in stressing over little things you can't do anything about, but I couldn't take my own advice.

I had the knowledge but I couldn't control my emotions. I started to worry that there was something seriously wrong with me physically, and when you're anxious your mind can go to very dark places.

I didn't really bother with myself when I wasn't at work. While I'd wash my hair every morning and get my hair and make-up done every weekday so I looked presentable, at weekends I would wear grey jogging bottoms and a T-shirt with my hair tied back.

Steve would say, 'Do you want to go out for a walk?' but all

I wanted to do was sit around in my tracksuit and wait until I felt better. My joggers were like a comfort blanket for me; I felt unsexy, undesirable and flat. I didn't feel good enough and I didn't feel like I fitted in anywhere. I certainly didn't feel like I deserved to be on TV every day.

Despite my newfound love of grey leisurewear, outwardly I must have appeared fine. People would tell me I looked well and no one knew there was anything wrong with me. I didn't know how to vocalise what I was feeling – how can you explain to people that you are losing control and losing yourself? I had a job to do, so there was no choice but to paint on a smile and be 'telly Lorraine'. I wasn't about to go on air and say to the nation: 'I didn't sleep well last night and I'm having a terrible time,' because people don't want to hear that.

The whole point of my television programme is that it's positive and inspirational. It is all about escapism and feeling good. It's a little oasis of happiness at the start of every weekday, and I was absolutely determined that no one would know what was going on behind the scenes. I didn't want people to look at me and think I was struggling; I wanted the show to feel upbeat.

I had to make a conscious effort to put myself in the zone and get through the show each day, and then I'd feel completely deflated afterwards. I was running on empty. It's difficult to look back and remember how dreadful it all was. It was genuinely hard to get out of my bed at times. I could see all the wonderful things in my life, I just couldn't appreciate them.

There were times when I would sit at home crying for hours, but somehow I was still functioning and going to work every day.

I felt like I was in a dark tunnel for about two years. It wasn't that I was miserable the whole time, sometimes I would come out of the darkness and feel more like myself. I'd get a rush of relief that the anxiety was passing, but then the next day I'd be back to square one. It was so frustrating not to have any control over it. One day I thought, 'What if this is just me now? Is this how I'm going to feel for the rest of my life?' I couldn't see a way out.

Steve and I talk a lot, and he had known for some time that something wasn't right. Things escalated when I started worrying about Rosie non-stop. We all worry about our kids, but I had never been in that state about her before. Steve encouraged me to see a doctor and eventually we realised that my menopause could have triggered this episode (I'll talk more about menopause later). I started on Hormone Replacement Therapy (HRT) and, with the support of Steve and friends, gradually I started to feel better. I was lucky that my anxiety responded so well to treatment, for many others it can be more complex.

Feeling anxious is part of the human condition, but when it takes over your life and leaves you frozen with pain and terror, you must take action. After experiencing anxiety, I have a better understanding of the condition, but comparing what I went through to what those who are seriously mentally unwell experience is like comparing a splinter in your finger to losing a hand.

The kind of anxiety that I, along with millions of others, feel can come from all sorts of places. There's the pressure we put on ourselves to be 'perfect', which I'll talk about later, and then there's the disturbing information and news that we're bombarded with on a daily basis that we need to understand how to handle.

We can't eradicate worry from our life completely, because problems will always come up. Life isn't all fluffy clouds and unicorns, and it's ok to put up your hand and ask for help when you feel like you're drowning.

Now when my mind starts whirring I have got much better at stopping the thoughts and telling myself I'm not going down that road. You can't live with that level of stress and anxiety. If you think it's going to tip you over the edge, you may need expert help. In an ideal world you need to stop the feeling before it gets to that point.

The NHS is incredible, but there are so many hoops to jump through in order to get help for mental health conditions, not to mention the interminable waiting lists – and that needs to change. A pal of mine was referred for grief counselling, but in order to get an appointment she was expected to fill out a long form online. She was so low that it felt too much for her, and I would imagine that's the case for a lot of people. If you're suffering from a serious mental health problem, something like filling out a long form is probably totally overwhelming, so how are you supposed to get the help you need? That's when people slip through the cracks.

But, thankfully, GPs aren't the only port of call. There are more and more services opening up in the UK all the time that offer help and support.

It could be that there's help available in your area that you don't even know about. I would always recommend that people look online for local services, whether it's for depression, anxiety or addiction issues, or even if you just need someone to chat to that day.

Some cafes and restaurants have even introduced sharing tables where you can go and sit and have a chat with other people who are on their own, which I think is a wonderful idea that helps people connect.

It goes without saying that if you or someone you know is ever feeling desperate, the emergency services are only a phone call away, as are the Samaritans. It's free to call or email the Samaritans and they're available 24/7, so there's always someone there to listen when you need them. They are genuine lifesavers.

It can be difficult to acknowledge that you need help – never mind asking for it. Those are huge steps, but they are the beginning of your way back. If you are having problems of your own, please don't be a stalwart; often when you're going through a bad time you can come across as being unsociable. Don't paint on a smile and say you're fine when your world is crashing down around your ears.

Everyone feels embarrassed and self-conscious at times. If it's your kid's first day at school and you're at the school gate, just say hello to another person and admit that you're a bit nervous or sad. You can bet that other people feel the same way. If you're feeling down, phone a pal and say, 'I need a chat. Can you listen to me or tell me a good joke?' Or get their opinion on something, you might find that you are getting worked up about nothing. Sometimes you just need someone else to tell

you you're worrying too much, or help you to get something into perspective.

Running problems past someone and just asking them, 'What do you think? Am I overreacting here?' can help to break it down. It's very easy to build things up in our heads and it can just take someone else to point out that it's really not a big deal. The worst thing you can do is shut down and shut people out, because worries fester and multiply. They have to come out somehow, and it's better that they do so on your terms.

EXERCISE

When you feel stress rising, think of the Rule of Five.

Either write down or list in your head: five things you can see,
four you can hear, three you can touch, two you can smell,
one you can taste. This simple exercise distracts from stress
and slows down racing thoughts.

5.   4.   3.   2.   1.

_____   _____   _____   _____   _____

_____   _____   _____   _____

_____   _____   _____

_____   _____

_____

BEING OPEN HAS HELPED ME THROUGH MY HARDEST TIMES

I'm an open book. I have kept a few subjects back for myself and my family – for instance, I wouldn't go on my show and openly discuss my sex life because Rosie would be mortified! But I am open about the major events in my life, like my miscarriage and my menopause. Being open about these experiences sparks conversations and connections, a process I find healing.

I had my miscarriage in 2001. I discovered I was pregnant in May and from the word go the pregnancy was very different from Rosie, who was five by this time. I hadn't suffered any morning sickness, but I felt queasy from the start and was completely exhausted. Steve and I decided not to tell anyone until I was past the three-month stage, and I carried on as normally as possible whilst feeling pretty ghastly most of the time.

Come June, we went to Oban, in Scotland, for a holiday. On the first day, while we were travelling, I got a stabbing pain in my right-hand side. The following morning I woke up at 4am feeling horrendous. I discovered I was bleeding quite a bit and it was obvious something wasn't right, so Steve and I drove all the way back home to a hospital in Dundee so I could have a scan. I had prepared myself for the worst but then the nurse said to me, 'There's something there. I think there's a heartbeat.'

I couldn't believe what I was hearing and I immediately started crying with relief. Sadly, the good news was short-lived.

I left hospital feeling positive, but that night I began bleeding again, and by the morning I was so weak that Steve phoned an ambulance. I was trying to pretend everything was ok in front of Rosie, but even she could tell that something was wrong and told me I looked 'white as a sheep' – bless her heart.

At the hospital, my worst fears were confirmed. I had miscarried at just over two months. I had to have an operation that morning and I was devastated.

As I lay in hospital, I questioned everything, wondering if I could have done something differently. One in three women will go through the agony of a miscarriage, which is a horrific statistic, but I had to do everything in my power not to blame myself. I felt so sad for Steve, too. We had both made plans for the future, and we'd been so excited about having a little brother or sister for Rosie.

Our family and friends were incredible and so supportive towards me, but I think partners can often be overlooked in that situation. Everyone was asking me how I was but very few people asked Steve how he was dealing with it. The people who did ask after him tended to be those who had been through something similar themselves.

I wanted to try to get back into a routine as quickly as possible following my miscarriage, to take my mind off things, but in retrospect I went back to work far too early and I didn't allow myself enough time to grieve. As a result, I would break down in tears in private regularly. If I saw a pram in the street or even saw someone on telly with a baby I would find tears rolling down my cheeks.

Three of my friends had babies later that year, and while it was hard, I was so overjoyed for them and I knew how lucky I was to have Rosie.

Steve and I didn't manage to have another baby, but I know I am very blessed. I've interviewed many women over the years who weren't able to have a child at all, and some who'd suffered the devastation of multiple miscarriages, and so I am very grateful.

People are so scared to say the wrong thing when a woman suffers a miscarriage or has a stillbirth that they don't say anything at all, and I do understand that. Everyone I've spoken to who has lost a baby just wants to acknowledge the existence of that child. That baby was very loved and is missed. It shouldn't be something we don't discuss or pretend didn't happen.

I decided to share my experience on air because I thought it might help other couples who were going through the same experience. I was amazed at the outpouring of sympathy and understanding. That support helped me through one of the most difficult times in my life.

When we go through traumatic experiences, our first instinct can be to hide ourselves away. In hard times, the very best thing you can do is to ask for help and be open with those closest to you.

POSITIVE THINKING

We're surrounded by negativity in the world and it's important that we stay as positive as we can. Even in my darkest times, I try very hard to find some light – sometimes that's just being grateful for another day above the ground. Shining can be about being thankful for the most obvious things.

If you're in the depths of despair, try to find something that makes you laugh – it might just be a YouTube clip of Billy Connolly performing – then create a folder or document full of links that are guaranteed to make you smile. You don't have to be bubbling over with happiness all the time because that's not realistic, but try to look right ahead to the end of the tunnel.

We can't usually do a lot about the terrible things that are going on in the world, but you can protect yourself by not getting sucked into the fear and darkness.

It's hard not to worry about terrorist attacks, for example, but we have to try to cut off from these fears, otherwise we'll be in a permanent state of stress and we give them power over us, which they do not deserve. The whole point of terrorism is to create fear, so we mustn't give them that. Try to put these fears into context; the probability of being caught up in such a disaster is remote.

Of course we need to be sensible and stay safe, but some things are out of our control and we have to accept that so we don't live in a permanent state of panic.

It's easy to be cynical and think the world is full of evil because we see a lot of terrible things happen, but we also need to remind ourselves that there are so many wonderful people out there, and there is joy and kindness. Our world is confusing and often scary and overwhelming, but it's also very beautiful.

Sometimes you need to make a conscious effort when you get up each day and think to yourself, 'Actually, I'm not going to be defined by negative thoughts.' Hold on to that and it becomes your reality, it really does. Positivity is a habit. It doesn't always come naturally and sometimes you have to make an effort until it becomes second nature.

Everything is relative. Sometimes you can shrug off negative thoughts, and at other times they will hit you like a ton of bricks. Of course, some of us are more sensitive than others. For instance, imagine you're shouted at by an aggressive driver on the road. You might forget about it a minute later. Or, if you have a more sensitive personality, the incident might play on your mind for days. We all react to things differently depending on our personality and history.

We see things through different filters, too. A friend of mine said that in her teens she remembers reading about a celebrity admitting to having addiction problems and was shocked they'd been so open about it and she had judged them for it. Fast-forward 30 years and she now respects honesty and bravery and would never judge someone for speaking out. We think about things in different ways not just because of who we are and our core beliefs, but because of what life teaches us as we get older.

If you're a sensitive person, chances are that while you might find day-to-day life difficult, you probably also have great intuition and empathy. Sometimes the negative parts of our personality are also our superpower.

EXERCISE

Make a list of your 'bad' characteristics and then consider how they might also contribute to the 'good' parts of your personality, too. Try to put a positive spin on each of your character traits, no matter how tiny they are. For example, some people might say I talk too much, but my ability to chatter no matter what is exactly what makes me good at my job!

I can be . . .

But that means I . . .

_____

_____

_____

_____

_____

_____

_____

_____

CHANGE YOUR MIND

If I wake up in the morning and I have an overwhelming, full-on day ahead of me it can be hard to motivate myself. Like everyone else, I'm only human. I have days where I go into work and have things playing on my mind and I don't feel like I'm on form. In fact, on days like those, I'd like to crawl straight back into bed and stay there until I feel better. If I'm finding it really hard to get out from under the duvet I will make a list of five things I'm looking forward to that day, even if it's just my mid-morning banana!

Every day I say to myself, 'It's another day and it's a fresh start and I'm going to go for this.' If things aren't going well I'll try to focus on the things that I can change.

If someone close to me is ill, I can't make them better but I can check in and see how they're doing. I ask myself, 'How can I make someone feel a bit better today?' Then I send them a daft text or a photo and hopefully make them smile. Exercise is also a really effective stress buster, so even when I think I'm too tired to go to my class I drag myself there, because I know I will feel so much better afterwards.

I'm lucky in the way that my show forces me to focus and compartmentalise, because no one wants to see me miserable at 8.30 in the morning. I am good at focusing on the job at hand and I love what I do, so for that hour I can forget about my other worries. I'm so busy while on air that I don't have time to think about whether Rosie's homesick or fret over my to-do list.

I have no choice but to pop the mind bubbles as they come up, otherwise I'd lose my train of thought as there's no space for them.

Adjusting your mindset is about accepting the things you can't or don't want to change and working on the things you can and want to, but without pushing yourself too hard. Never forget that life is here to be enjoyed.

To be genuinely happy we must accept the things we want to change and work on them. I'm aware of my downfalls. I know I can be very impatient. I do things too quickly and I rush them and I'm not as methodical as I could be. I'm also too neat, to the point where I sometimes tidy up my close friends' houses when I go round (I've been known to rearrange ornaments so they're more uniform, or put books in alphabetical order because it makes me feel better. Who does that?!).

I'm terrible at finishing people's sentences for them, too, or I talk to them like I'm interviewing them. That's probably because I generally have six minutes to get the best out of someone on the show and it spills into everyday life. I wasn't aware of doing this when I was younger, but now I watch it. It's not a terrible shortcoming, and it's part of what makes me me, but I know it can be annoying, so I'm working on it.

It sounds terribly simple, but concentrating on the things that you have control over helps to occupy your mind and stop you thinking about the things you want to change but can't for whatever reason. You have to put yourself in a good state of mind. If you say positive things to yourself often enough you do start to believe them. Even if it's just saying 'I'm doing fine'.

We're so bad at taking compliments, but start consciously giving them to yourself until it becomes the norm.

You can't run away from your problems, but you can learn to face them better by counting your blessings. It's such an old-fashioned term but there's a reason why it's still said by so many people every single day, and why people still do it!

So many of the oldest sayings around still ring true, such as:

- *Do as you would be done by.*

- *Think before you speak.*

- *If you don't have anything nice to say about someone, don't say anything at all.*

- *You can't please all of the people all of the time.*

- *Don't mix light and dark spirits. (This one is very important!)*

EXERCISE

Just for today, try to concentrate on the 'can dos' rather than the 'cannots'. Write down a list of all the things that are tricky in your life right now, then separate them into things you can change and things you can't. Now focus on what you can change and come up with strategies to solve them. If you're struggling to think of a solution, is there someone you could ask for help?

Problem: _____

Can I change it? _____

How can I change it? _____

Who can help? _____

HAPPINESS STARTS WITH A HEALTHY MIND

Lorri Craig is a registered psychologist and AIT practitioner who has over 30 years' experience of treating people with anxiety, depression and other mental health problems. Here she answers some key questions.

How is depression defined?

Most of us feel low or sad at times, but that doesn't mean we all have a diagnosable form of depression. Clinical depression, or major depressive disorder, lasts for at least a couple of weeks, and often lasts for months. It can be very debilitating and can make it hard for sufferers to get out of bed or go to work. According to the World Health Organization, depression is the leading cause of ill health and disability in the world.

Symptoms of depression can include:

- *Low mood*
- *Apathy*
- *Feeling worthless and hopeless*
- *Feeling emotionless and detached*
- *Feeling excessively tearful and overwhelmed*
- *Difficulty concentrating*
- *Disordered sleep*
- *Suicidal thoughts*

There is a difference between depression and grief. They can have very similar symptoms but grief is, of course, a normal reaction to the loss of a loved one. However, when those emotions get stuck they can lead to depression.

If a woman develops depression during a pregnancy or within the first year after giving birth it's called post-partum or post-natal depression, but that's not the same as the day or two of tearfulness that women might get immediately after giving birth as a result of changes in hormones. That reaction is often referred to as the 'baby blues', whereas post-natal depression is a chronic form of depression.

How about anxiety? What are the main symptoms of that?

Anxiety is also very common and can also be debilitating. It's normal to worry and feel anxious about things, but when someone has an anxiety disorder it impinges on their everyday life.

Symptoms of general anxiety disorder can include:

- *Panic attacks*

- *Shaking and trembling*

- *Muscle tension*

- *Restlessness and agitation*

- *A sense of doom*

- *Racing, out-of-control thoughts that catastrophise everything*

- *Feeling afraid and not being able to rationalise how you're feeling*

- *Difficulty concentrating*

- *Difficulty sleeping*

Generalised anxiety is the most common type of anxiety disorder, but there are others, including:

- *Social anxiety, which is feeling excessive fear in social situations*
- *Phobia disorder, in which you irrationally fear a specific thing*
- *Obsessive compulsive disorder, in which you obsessively do something to the degree that it impacts on your life*
- *Panic disorder, where you have frequent panic attacks*
- *Post trauma stress disorder, in which you are debilitated by the reliving of a severe traumatic event*

Depression and anxiety sound very similar in some ways?

It's not uncommon for people to have both. When we feel threatened in any way, our body goes into the 'fight or flight' response. This means that it instantly releases stress hormones which make our heart rate and blood pressure go up, we breathe more quickly, and our muscles tense up so we're ready to run or fight off the danger. This was helpful if we were facing a wild animal in primitive times, but in the modern world there are many things our brains perceive as dangerous that we can't run away from or fight, such as deadlines, or losing a job, or feeling judged by people. These stressors can increase the stress hormones in our body in a chronic way. And of course, the conversations and distorted visualisations in our imagination often magnify our distress.

Anxiety is the pure manifestation of the 'fight or flight' response that won't switch off, or is triggered too easily – like a smoke detector that goes off every time you cook toast. Depression comes from the system becoming exhausted and overwhelmed and deprived of the happy hormones that we get when we are not stressed.

Are some people more prone to mental illness?

Some people have more stressors and bad experiences to deal with, and some people are better at processing experiences than others. Some people's brains may simply not produce enough 'happy hormones'.

We are more vulnerable if a bunch of stressful or difficult things happen at once, or if unprocessed traumatic experiences build up over time. Depression and anxiety do tend to run in families, but studies show that environmental factors play an even bigger part than genetics. This includes how you were brought up, and the way your parents reacted to problems and life in general. So, genetics and traumas aside, if your parents were calm and positive, you are going to find it easier to be calm and positive in your adult life.

How can we keep on top of our mental health?

It's about learning to manage the stress and our body and mind's reaction to it so it doesn't get out of control, whether that's through relaxation, exercise, talking or taking actions to change your situation.

What's the first thing we should do if we're feeling anxious or panicky?

Remember to breathe OUT. If we were being chased by a wild animal in the wilderness and we made it safely to our cave where the creature couldn't reach us, what would we do? We'd let our breath go with a sigh of relief. So breathe out and relax your body as you do so, to trick your primitive brain into thinking that you are safe in your cave. That reduces your stress hormones and increases your relaxing happy hormones. Emptying our lungs allows more room for new air which helps to alleviate the feeling of breathlessness. Slowing and relaxing our breathing can reduce the weird fuzzy sensation that comes from over-breathing or hyperventilation. Simply focusing on your breath helps to calm the nervous system.

If you have a panic attack, your heart is racing and you feel like you can't breathe, then try this technique:

- *Breathe out to the count of four, focusing on your breath, and hold it for a second.*

- *Breathe in for a count of two and hold it for a second. Try to breathe gently into your abdomen.*

- *Repeat for as long as you need to.*

Stress can also have a huge effect on our physical health, can't it?

Chronic stress is really bad for our physical health. Every single structure and system in our body is badly affected by chronic stress. It affects our cardiovascular, hormone, digestive, immune and nervous systems, which is why using calming and relaxing techniques is so important, even if we don't feel particularly stressed.

But as you mentioned, modern life is stressful, so it's difficult not to feel under pressure or het up sometimes.

To a certain extent, we have to choose how we want to feel. If another driver cuts you up, it's natural to feel a surge of fear and even anger in response. But if you hold on to your anger, and feed it with your judgemental thoughts, you're the one who's left feeling stressed. Instead, breathe out, relax and let it go.

Think about how you usually feel in difficult situations. Every time you hold on to anger, worry or guilt, you hurt yourself. We're all human and we make mistakes and we have to assume that's going to happen and do our best to let it pass when it does. It's important to be aware of how we're feeling and do our best to change it if it's not serving us.

We need to love and be kind to ourselves in spite of our mistakes. It may sound a bit clichéd, but imagine sending yourself lots of love whenever you're stressed, sad or worried. It's the small emotional child inside who is upset, so getting cross with her won't make her or you feel better. But, equally, allowing her to wallow is not the best idea either. Acknowledge your feelings, comfort yourself, then distract yourself, as you would a young child.

How can we release anger?

You can use the same stress management and relaxation techniques as above. Body combat and martial art practices can be particularly helpful. It can also be good to shout and scream in the car with the windows up, in a safe and private place!

Is there a good way to put the brake on once the anxiety or depression merry-go-round starts?

It works differently for different people, but the bottom line is finding ways to give yourself a rest from all that negative thinking about the past and the future, and find a way to trick your primitive brain into believing that there is no threat and that you've metaphorically found your safe cave.

Some good tips are:

- *Don't push the feelings away. Accept them but then turn your attention away from the thoughts that make you feel bad to thoughts that make you feel better.*

- *Give your mind something else to focus on, whether it's a book, game, TV show, or something around you.*

- *Practise mindfulness. Be more present in the moment to take your attention away from the thoughts in your head. Notice the sounds and smells around you. Really listen for every tiny noise. Focus your attention on to a nearby plant or pen or a piece of furniture and notice its colours and patterns. Hold an apple in your hand, smell it, and feel its texture.*

- *Exercise. It really is the best medicine and will release built-up tension. It both tricks the mind into thinking that you have run from danger and so are safe, and helps you to move your attention from your mind to your body. Don't wait until you feel like doing it. Just do it.*

- *Sip a glass of water really slowly and focus on it going into your body. By the time you finish the glass, your body and mind will have had a chance to calm down.*

- *Bring yourself back into your body and into the present by focusing on relaxing with the out-breath in your belly.*

- *Clean the house or car. Declutter and clear out cupboards.*

- *Listen to relaxing music.*

- *Sing and dance.*

- *Do some gardening.*

- *Get a massage.*

- *Do something thoughtful for someone else.*

- *Cuddle or have sex with your partner!*

- *Talk. Pick up the phone and call someone.*

- *Socialise. An interest group such as biking, gardening or painting can be a good way to connect with people. Meetup is a good site to find groups on anything and everything. There are even meet-up groups for people with anxiety and depression. And you know that if you've found it hard to walk through that door, so has everyone else.*

- *Meditate. Listen to a mindfulness meditation or guided relaxation session via YouTube or an app, or go to a meditation centre to learn techniques.*

- *Look upwards more, with your shoulders back (but be careful when walking around roads!).*

- *Colour, draw, paint, knit, sew or do pottery or a jigsaw puzzle.*

- *Play a sport.*

- *Get out in nature.*

- *Try doing something scary, like riding on a rollercoaster, climbing a tree or rock climbing. This will make your stress hormones peak initially, but the relief of being safe afterwards can boost happy hormones.*

- *Avoid too much alcohol and other relaxing drugs. They can give temporary relief, but anything that gives quick relief usually results in us feeling worse later on.*

- *Talk to a professional psychologist, psychotherapist or counsellor.*

It's great that we're talking about mental illness so much more now, and seeking help. It's gradually becoming less taboo and more socially acceptable to open up. People like Ruby Wax and Princes Harry and William have helped with that.

What's your advice for people who have trouble sleeping?

Not sleeping is almost always to do with overthinking. It can be hard because when you can't sleep you inevitably start worrying about the impact of not sleeping.

- *Take your attention away from your mind by focusing on your body. Begin by taking two or three really deep breaths where you relax your body with the out-breath.*

- *Envision a gentle sensation moving down through the top of your head and all the way down your body and out through the soles of your feet.*

- *Focus on your breath in your belly, but allow it to be light and gentle with a gap between the out-breath and the in-breath.*

- *It can be helpful to occupy the verbal part of your brain by counting your out-breaths backwards, so you can start at 50 and count down to 10, and then repeat.*

- *Alternatively, say a mantra over and over again. The best ones are nonsense phrases like 'om ee way oh om' that don't mean anything. Create your own and repeat it over and over again. Your mind will try and take you back to your worries, but keep bringing it back to your mantra.*

- *If you're a visual person, you can imagine a pattern of something like leaves falling down or a pulsing star, and focus on that. Again, keep coming back to it when your mind tries to take you back to your racing thoughts.*

Have you got any tips for improving self-esteem?

The bottom line is: be nice to yourself! When we see a beautiful, magnificent tree, we don't go up to it and start looking for flaws, we appreciate the tree as an amazing being. We need to do that for ourselves. We need to take a step back and appreciate ourselves as a whole instead of focusing on any small perceived flaws. Imagine if we could love the whole of us, insecurities and all. What power! Be kind to and praise that little kid inside you. Carl Rogers, a famous therapist, once said, 'The curious paradox is that when I accept myself just as I am, then I can change.'

It can be helpful to write a list of all the things you appreciate about yourself, including aspects of your body and personality, as well as your achievements. Try to add something to the list and read the whole thing aloud every day. A lovely thing to do is to go around and ask all the people you love and trust to tell you something they like about you and add those comments to your list.

And how about relationship advice?

A relationship is a bit like a ship sailing the ocean. There are smooth, easy times, rough times, and even the odd storm, so we have to try to navigate carefully, enjoy the smooth and the rough times and ride out the storms. Here are my top tips:

- *Mutual respect is the most important thing, above anything else.*

- *Let some disagreements go and choose your battles. As someone once wisely said, 'I'd rather be happy than right.'*

- *Having the guts to sincerely apologise for our own part in a problem can be a powerful remedy.*

- *Accept and forgive other people's human flaws as well as your own.*

- *Show affection often. A hug goes a long way.*

Finally, what are the main types of therapy that are on offer for people who are suffering with mental health problems, and how can we find a good therapist?

Charities such as Sane and Mind have great resources. There are a few different websites, like the BACP (British Association for Counselling and Psychotherapy), UKCP (UK Council for Psychotherapists) and the BPS (British Psychological Society), where you can find accredited psychological therapists. Psychologists, like me, must be registered through the government HCPC (Health and Care Professionals Council). The HCPC doesn't offer a directory service, but you can check their register to make sure someone is registered.

Good old Google can be helpful for finding services and private practitioners near you. I would recommend using your instincts when you look at someone's website and biog. If possible, have a quick chat with them over the phone before you go and see them to make sure you feel comfortable with them. Online and email therapy are also options now, so your therapist doesn't necessarily have to live near you if you're happy to work in that way.

Some of the main therapies on offer:

- *CBT (Cognitive Behaviour Therapy) is the therapy offered most often by all the government-funded services. It focuses on changing behaviours and the thoughts that trigger us; for instance, by challenging those thoughts.*

- *Mindfulness-based CBT and ACT (Acceptance and Commitment Therapy) encourages us to relax and accept our thoughts and feelings, rather than getting caught up in them.*

- *Psychodynamic psychotherapy helps clients to identify and process past experiences that have contributed to their psychological issues.*

- *Psycho-physical or energy psychology therapies like EFT (Emotional Freedom Technique), EMDR (Eye Movement Desensitisation and Reprocessing) and AIT (Advanced Integrative Therapy) are very effective in clearing those traumatic experiences quickly and gently. They incorporate the body into the treatment because we feel and hold emotions and tension in our body, not just in our mind. In AIT we also clear the presenting symptoms and the links between the past and present. This clears out traumas and emotions that are stuck and automatically reduces the overflow of symptoms, such as anxiety and depression.*

CONFIDENCE

Confidence can mean the difference between biting the bullet and going for what you want or playing it safe and never achieving your goals. And let's face it, if you never try in life, you never know. You don't want to look back and regret missing chances because you were too scared to take a risk.

IT'S ALL ABOUT THE CONFIDENCE

Confidence is tricky. I wouldn't say I'm the most confident person in the world, but I've certainly got more confident as I've got older. Being loved makes you more confident, and I don't just mean by your partner, but by friends and family, too.

As a nation, we're not very good at saying that we love each other. Sometimes it can take someone being ill before we open up and tell them we love them. Not everybody is the same but, by and large, we don't say it enough.

I wasn't particularly confident growing up. I was bullied at school and felt incredibly out of place as a result. It started when I was about seven or eight. Even though the area of Glasgow I came from was very poor, my mum still turned me out like a little princess. She would tie my hair up in cut-up bits of old tights the night before school, then take them out in the morning so I had tight ringlets. Then she'd add bows and put me in a pink dress. She took pride in my appearance, but this get-up made me stand out from the others. I may as well have gone around with a sign on my back saying 'kick me'! I got picked on because people thought I was posh, but it was only because my dad worked so hard that we were able to buy decent clothes and a home that my mum turned into a little palace.

The fact that I could read and write early and was a bit of a swot didn't help, so I used to dumb myself down and refuse to put my hand up in class and answer questions in case there were repercussions.

In the end, the bullying got so bad I told my parents about it – which of course I should have done straight away instead of waiting for it to spiral out of control. My mum was so worried about me she planned to go and speak to my teacher. However, my Auntie Carol – who is 10 years older than me – found out, so she marched straight up to my school and threatened to kick the backsides of the girls who were bullying me. I would not recommend it as a way to resolve matters, but it did work. My teacher was appalled when she found out about the bullying and looked out for me after that.

The saddest thing about being bullied was that it made me try to fit in more as a result. It took away a bit of my individuality. I was so desperate to blend in that I tried to conform and become invisible for a while. Thankfully, once the bullying stopped, I eventually made friends and found myself again.

After I left school, I made lots of fantastic gay pals in Glasgow – and that changed me as a person all over again. I discovered a group of people who were seen as a bit strange and quirky like me, and who didn't necessarily conform, and I felt like I'd finally found my place.

In retrospect, I'm grateful for the bullying experience because it made me understand what it's like not to feel included. It helped me to appreciate people's differences. Later in life, when my friends were gay or transitioning, or they felt different in some way, I understood a bit of what they were going through.

For me, being bullied created an affinity with people who are slightly outside of things, because I've always felt that way myself. I know that sounds silly when I do the job that I do, but I can be a bit of a loner. Even when I joined *TV-am*, we were on the outside of the established broadcast media. We were like the kids who had our noses pressed up against the window of the party and weren't allowed in and I still feel a bit like that.

Finding your clan really does give you confidence. If you meet other people who think like you, have the same sense of humour and give you support and love no matter what, then you feel like you belong. Do you think you've already found yours, or is it time to start looking for them?

Confidence comes from being appreciated, and from letting your barriers down and allowing people to see your vulnerabilities. We all want to be liked, and sometimes we put on a face to the world to make that happen. But accepting that you are loveable because of your flaws – and not despite them – is crucial. The right people will love you, warts and all.

Not everyone has a supportive family, but sometimes you can create your own family of amazing friends. I could really relate to the brilliant TV series, *Pose*, which illustrates beautifully how when people are shunned by their own family due to their sexuality or lifestyle they can find their own clan. You don't necessarily need to be related to be a family.

Confidence also comes from overcoming tough times, whether it's being bullied or having a terrible tragedy in your life. Being able to cope with that, and realising that what doesn't kill you makes you stronger, shows you what you're capable of. When you're tested you often find you can get through something using your inner strength, and also by drawing on the people around you, and then when you come out the other side something inside of you shifts a little bit.

I used to fret a lot more than I do now. I was always thinking 'I could have done that better'. I would find the smallest thing to worry about, and I wouldn't see the bigger picture when I'd done something well. Imagine you have two hungry dogs inside of you. One of them is your confident side and the other is the insecure part of you. If you keep feeding the insecure dog with negativity, he's going to get bigger and become dominant. Whereas if you feed the positive one with kind words and self-care, it will grow larger and be in charge.

EXERCISE

List 25 of your best qualities and achievements. It might seem like a lot, but give it a go. It could be simple things like the fact that your kids know they're loved, or your loyalty to your friends. These things are what make you remarkable. If you can't stop at 25, keep going!

1. _____

2. _____

3. _____

4. _____

5. _____

6. _____

7. _____

8. _____

9. _____

10. _____

11. _____

12. _____

13. _____

14. _____

15. _____

16. _____

17. _____

18. _____

19. _____

20. _____

21. _____

22. _____

23. _____

24. _____

25. _____

NOT EVERYONE IS GOING TO LIKE YOU

I know this is tough to hear, but you're just not going to be everyone's cup of tea. Wanting to be popular and liked is normal and human, but the reality is that it's impossible to be universally loved, and with social media you can get a thumbs down from someone who doesn't know a thing about you.

Some people aren't going to like you no matter how nice you are or how hard you try. Even the most beautiful people in the world, or those going through terrible times and who are in need of comfort, will sadly be subjected to abuse.

Now let out a long sigh of relief as that realisation sinks in. It feels good to let go of that expectation, doesn't it? You're not a failure just because you rub someone up the wrong way. We take it way too much to heart.

I can be as guilty as the next person of caring too much about what other people think. It's like the episode of *Frasier* when he's watching a focus group and there's one person who isn't all that keen on him and his radio show. He becomes fixated on him to the point that he tracks him down and the guy just says, 'I'm sorry, I just don't like you.' Sometimes it can be as simple as that. Frasier and his fragile ego end up turning this rejection into a much bigger deal than it needs to be (eventually through a series of hilarious mishaps Frasier ends up burning down the poor man's tobacco kiosk. A little bit of an overreaction…), when he really should just have accepted it and moved on.

You can't be all things to all people, and you will drive yourself mad trying. It's taken me a long time to stop trying to please everyone. I've realised you have to be a pretty pathetic person to go out of your way to tell people you don't like them, whether that is in person (rare) or via social media (the cowardly way). I've gone from being deeply hurt to the point of tears to feeling sorry for them, because it must be really awful being them.

I'M NOT PERFECT, AND NEITHER ARE YOU!

Let's get one thing straight: no one, and I mean no one, is perfect. Perfection is a big old myth and even the word annoys me; it's something that doesn't exist. We make ourselves unhappy by chasing a fantasy.

The biggest lesson I've learned is that while buying a fabulous handbag is wonderful, material things are fleeting, and as naff as it sounds, it's feeling happy and peaceful inside that truly makes us feel good day after day.

Things may look glossy in my world, and I know some people see me as this golden girl because I'm on telly and smile a lot, but it makes me laugh because I've had struggles just like everyone else. I've had my fair share of let-downs, knockbacks and things to overcome, but they've all made me who I am today and I wouldn't change a thing. There really is no point in regret or wondering if things could have turned out differently. The past is the past, and the present and future are what's important, and what matters most is how we can make them our best times yet. When you go through the ups and downs you come out the other side with more knowledge and wisdom, so I always try to remember that, no matter how bad things are.

Of course, there are days when we don't want to be grateful for the tough times. Sometimes things just feel awful. And do you know what? That's ok, because we're all human. Giving yourself a hard time is not going to help; it only makes everything worse. In these situations I remind myself that I am not infallible and things can and will get on top of me. We are so tough on ourselves, constantly thinking, 'I should have done that' or 'I shouldn't have said that'. What a waste of energy! It's good to learn from your mistakes, but don't berate yourself over them. There's nothing wrong with self-improvement, but self-loathing is deeply harmful.

You are not superwoman, and that's ok. Imagine what a boring world it would be if we were all wafting around being perfect. We all have flaws; not one person I know loves everything about themselves, which is sad. Imagine how much happier we would all be if we could accept ourselves just as we are? We often fixate on the small things that we perceive to be wrong with us and waste time worrying about them. What a shame when we could use that energy for more positive things.

Society is built on our insecurities. The beauty and fashion industries exist to sell us products. Advertising gives the impression that these products will give us the perfect look and the perfect life. But it's all temporary; you can't hinge your self-esteem on external factors. Even the brightest and best version of yourself won't meet these unrealistic standards.

The same goes for the way we think about our bodies. I have so much more self-acceptance these days because I have finally made peace with the fact that this is who I am, and my flaws are just fine.

When we did the 'The Bikini Promise' on the show in 2015 (where I wanted women to embrace their bodies and feel confident no matter what age, shape or size they were), I was filmed dancing in my bikini outside the studio with all of the team and the viewers who had taken part. There were some photos taken, too, and I refused to allow them to be airbrushed. Some people actually accused me of Photoshopping those bikini pics because one of my legs was a bit wonky, which is often a tell-tale sign, but the big bump in my thigh was actually my scar from my horse-riding accident (more about that later).

When I released my fitness DVD with Maxine Jones, I was determined that it would be completely authentic, with no Photoshopping on the cover. I agreed to do the DVD on the proviso that we filmed one of Maxine's classes with everyone who normally goes along. I wanted it to be real and authentic and to give everyone a chance to experience all that sheer joy and energy. We were hot, sweaty and we looked dishevelled, just as we always do. I was totally myself, complete with a glowing red face, and I honestly think that's why the DVD did so well.

It's about time we got real. I never edit my selfies and I'm happy to be seen as I really am. I wouldn't even know how to put a shiny filter over a photo of myself to give me a wrinkle-free face like a boiled egg. It's become a tradition that every week after her class Maxine and I take a selfie. I always look a bit messy and bedraggled but it doesn't bother me one bit.

I did an interview for a magazine a little while ago and the journalist said, 'It's terrible that you post those awful pictures. It's really bad for your image.' Well, firstly I don't have an image. And secondly, that's what women look like when they exercise.

There was a survey done recently where women said they wouldn't go to the gym because they don't want to look hot and sweaty. What a terrible shame that's stopping them from being happy and healthy. If you want to look better in the long term, you're going to have to spend time looking less than perfect. If you're that worried about looking dishevelled you can always work out at home – there are plenty of workouts available on DVD or online that you can follow.

We've all seen those people who go along to the gym dressed up in the latest gear, with a full face of make-up, then walk at a snail's pace on the treadmill while they watch MTV in case (heaven forfend) they should break into a sweat. What the hell? What is the point? It's bonkers. You're working out, not attending a cocktail party.

I do worry about all of the fakery of images on social media and the way that 'flawless' photos make people, especially young girls, feel about themselves. I loved how outraged Kate Winslet was when a men's magazine Photoshopped her legs to look thinner. She commented at the time, 'I do not look like that and, more importantly, I don't desire to look like that.' She also had a no-retouching clause when she landed a big campaign with L'Oréal, and said, 'We're all responsible for raising strong young women, so these are things that are so important to me.'

I also remember interviewing Cindy Crawford a few years back and she told me she's seen magazine covers where she didn't even recognise herself. They had airbrushed her to such an extent it could have been anyone staring back at her. Even someone that beautiful isn't immune from a designer's airbrush.

Far too many young people don't have the ability to step back and realise that what they see online and on magazine covers just isn't real, and that worries me.

There are some fascinating examples of before and after airbrushing online. In fact, there are whole Instagram accounts dedicated to them. They're a good way to get a reality check and help you to see the refreshing truth behind the (not really perfect!) pictures. So check them out – I promise you will feel better.

BE A BIT MORE PIERS MORGAN (YES, REALLY)

At one time, if someone told me they liked my dress I'd reply, 'Oh, this old thing, it only cost a tenner.' I could never just accept a compliment. I didn't think I was all that worthy of other people's praise, which many of us are guilty of. We should be able to say, 'Thanks, that's really good of you,' and appreciate their kind words.

I'm less apologetic these days but I was always slightly sorry for everything I did. I had this working-class cringe and felt like I was going to get found out and frogmarched out of the door.

I always remember someone saying to Billy Connolly that he'd lost all sense of where he came from when he was hanging out with Royals, to which he quite rightly replied, 'What am I supposed to do? Am I supposed to say, "I'm sorry, I can't possibly come to the palace because I'm too working class"?'

Do we need to apologise 20 times a day? No! Let's start noticing how many times we apologise and work on cutting down. A genuine apology means the world, but saying sorry when someone accidentally treads on our toe? That's daft.

I wish I cared less about what other people think, but I am working on it. One of the traits I hate most in people is selfishness, which is often tied in with not caring about what anyone else thinks. That can take you down a bad road, but on the flip side, you can care way too much, and I am guilty of that at times. You need to strike a good balance, which isn't easy.

I would love to have more of a 'whatever' attitude, but unless you're Piers Morgan, we all care what others think about us. Piers, on the other hand, genuinely doesn't care what people think about him, and it's admirable in many ways (but don't ever tell him I've said that). He gets some shocking insults on social media and merrily reposts them, gleefully correcting the trolls' bad spelling.

Such resilience is a skill, and it is something you can learn. I don't think my skin will ever be as thick as Piers' is, and I will always be a sensitive soul, but I am becoming more resilient simply because I'm more content within myself.

PRACTISE COMPASSION

Compassion is essential, whether we're showing it to ourselves or to others (ideally, both, and often!). It's so important that we find little ways to be kinder every day. That's when we truly shine.

THE DANGER OF COMPARISON-ITIS

Comparing yourself with others is so destructive and will only make you miserable. One minute you're having a perfectly good time, the next you're down a bottomless social media well and you're wondering why you're not lying on a beach in Jamaica drinking a colourful cocktail.

Don't. Compare. Yourself. To. Anyone. It's a hiding to nothing.

That woman who looks ecstatic in a photo of her sipping a Tequila Sunrise isn't going to tell you that her plane was delayed for seven hours, or that she's got a dodgy tummy from overdoing things. Do away with FOMO (Fear Of Missing Out). Don't for a minute think that everyone else in the world is having fun apart from you. Social media is a highlights reel; it's not real life. We've all got that friend who will post a photo of themselves having the time of their life one minute, then phone you up crying the next. You don't know what's going on behind a photograph.

We naturally compare ourselves to the people around us, but comparing yourself to celebrities is the worst thing to do because it's their job to look like they're the luckiest people in the world. I've always found the likes of Tom Hanks, Oprah Winfrey and Will Smith will be a total delight even on their umpteenth interview of the day because they're professionals.

That said, sometimes I interview people and I know they're thinking, 'I just don't want to be here.' It's written all over their face. Someone has bought their clothes and done their hair and make-up to make them look gorgeous, and they've got the entire floor of the poshest hotel in London to themselves, but maybe they've got to sit there and talk about a movie they don't really like and would rather be at home having a beer with their pals.

We're all unique. We all have good and bad qualities; perhaps one of us might have beautiful eyes while another may have an amazing bottom, so it's pointless trying to be like someone else. You're not them! Absolutely everyone has hang-ups no matter how gorgeous they are, and that's ok.

Nobody, and I mean nobody, is perfect. Being beautiful doesn't make you invincible either, even the likes of Naomi Campbell or Gigi Hadid will have lost out on jobs to other models. I'm sure when that happens they will question why and wobble a bit.

Even if you are the funniest or most beautiful person in the world, you will probably always think someone is better than you, and that's not going to do your self-esteem any favours.

NO ONE IS BETTER OR WORSE THAN ANYONE ELSE

I've always treated people the same: rich, poor, gay, straight, whatever you look like, wherever you're from, it doesn't matter. I remember my old boss at *TV-am* said to me one day, 'I love the fact that this morning you were talking to the Weight Watchers' slimmer of the year and Richard Branson in exactly the same way.'

Yes, Richard Branson deserves respect for working hard and becoming such a success, but so did that lovely woman who had lost eight stone. Everyone deserves to be treated with kindness and respect, whether they have five pounds or five billion pounds to their name.

You never know what's going on in people's lives. You don't know their story. When you see a homeless person you don't know how they ended up living rough. It's said that many people are just three pay packets away from being on the streets, and by no fault of their own they can end up penniless and without help. We can be quick to criticise and judge, but we haven't walked in their shoes and we don't know what they've been through.

Enjoying other people's downfall or looking down on them

won't get you anywhere, either. Crowing over someone else's bad fortune is mean-spirited, and if you find yourself doing that, consider why. Envy will eat away at you and nothing positive will come out of it.

If something hasn't worked out or someone has fallen from grace, at least they've tried. You don't know what else is going on in their lives. You don't know what outside factors have influenced what's happened to them, so show a bit of compassion.

In this country, we are terrible for building people up to knock them down, and it's so destructive. Everyone's just trying to live their lives and find their place in the world. As long as they're not committing crimes or hurting anyone, what's the problem?

One of the qualities that I value most in myself is that I don't judge others. It's too easy to take the moral high ground. I don't understand why people get such a buzz from putting other people down or why people get so riled up about things that are nothing to do with them. Why would somebody take offence at two women or two men getting married? What's it got to do with you, and how is it going to affect you?

All you should want is for people to be happy. I don't care how hippy dippy it sounds, if we were all as quick to love as we are to judge other people, the world would be a much better place.

I know it's become a bit of a buzz phrase now but, my advice? Stop worrying about what other people are doing and focus on being the best version of you.

EXERCISE

Think of the three people you dislike the most. Now think of three genuine compliments for each of them. You may have to dig pretty deep, but everyone has good qualities if you look hard enough.

FINDING CALM IN A FRANTIC WORLD

I think one of the biggest challenges facing all of us every day is finding time. Busyness leads to exhaustion, stress and, if you're not careful, you can lose your sense of self – your spark! If having five minutes to yourself feels like a luxury, you're losing the time war. It's time to put up a fight!

THANKS, BUT NO THANKS

I have a terrible but common habit of being a people-pleaser. I tell people what they want to hear – and that's not good for anyone. It was like second nature until a few years ago, but now it's something I pick myself up on and I'm trying to say 'no' more.

There was a time when I'd say yes to everything and as a result would be pulled in a hundred different directions. Eventually, I would realise that I'd said yes to too much and would get into a terrible tizzy. As soon as things calmed down a bit, I'd go and do it all again. The bottom line is, I just want to do the right thing, but sometimes you just have to say no.

In the past, if someone asked me to go to an event I would say yes without checking my diary. In my head I would say 'No I can't!', then I'd open my mouth and 'Yes' would come out.

Inevitably, I would double-book myself, end up letting people down and then get really upset about it. I've become better at pausing before I agree to things now; I concentrate on working with two or three charities and do as much as I possibly can for them. Anything else I can fit in is a bonus.

Some people expect too much of others and as a result they're constantly disappointed. Whether it's someone asking you to feed their cats or look after their kids, be careful not to spread yourself too thin or to let other people take advantage of your generosity.

It's too easy to say yes to things months in advance, then all of a sudden the event you've agreed to is looming, and you really don't want to do it. Then you get in a right old pickle because you've got to try to get out of it.

Sometimes you don't even have time to do all the things you need to do for yourself, and yet you take on other people's chores. It goes a long way just to be honest in a really positive way and say, 'You know I would help if I could and I've helped in the past, but I can't right now. I hope you understand.' If they don't understand, they don't have your best interests at heart and they're just using you. If they don't ever speak to you again, maybe that's not such a terrible thing? It's a shame, but you've got to manage expectations both for yourself and other people.

You don't want to be the person that everyone dumps on, but you don't want to be selfish either. It's about balance and honesty and not feeling coerced. The first time you say no you will probably feel terrible and worry about what they will think, but give it a couple of days to settle down and it will get easier, and I bet you will feel really proud that you stood up for yourself.

I'm not suggesting that we all stop helping each other, because that would be truly awful, but there's nothing wrong with having boundaries or taking the time to work out if you're doing a favour for the right reason. Are you doing something because you want everyone to think you're a great person, or do you genuinely want to help out?

There will be a period of adjustment if you've always been the person that said yes to everything. The minute you take a stand, some people won't like it. It may take them a little while to get used to the new way of doing things, so be prepared for that. We have to value ourselves and show people how we want to be treated.

When you're invited to something, think, 'If that event was happening tomorrow, would I want to do it?' Things seem more appealing and doable when they're ages away. If you get an email or text invite, don't reply right away, take some time to think about it first. If someone asks you face-to-face, don't panic and agree to something you're not sure about, say that you need to check and get back to them. That gives you time to work out whether it's something you want to do or not.

EXERCISE

What do you always agree to that you regret later? Practise saying
no. Work out exactly what you would say and how you would say it.
Write it down to help you remember.

_____

_____

_____

_____

_____

_____

_____

TAKE TIME

I am a bit obsessed with timing. I'm always far too early for any event and Steve has to remind me that no one is going to tell me off if I'm five minutes late. I think it's down to my job; my show is live – it starts at 8.30am and ends at 9.25am – and I cannot, under any circumstances, be late.

One sign that I'm under too much stress is my horrible recurring dream: I'm late getting to the studio, and then I can't find the way in. I'm banging on the door in my pyjamas with wet hair and no make-up, and the clock is counting down the seconds until we're on air. It's always very vivid and I wake up in a right old panic.

We rush around and get stressed and we don't leave ourselves enough time, which means we get even more het up. I always try to allow extra time to get to places so I don't feel anxious, but life doesn't always go to plan, and I remind myself that the world isn't going to end if I miss a train, bus or plane. Traffic jams happen, buses get delayed and people understand. File 'being late' in that box of things you're not going to waste your energy on!

That said, to-do lists help me stay organised and keep to a schedule. I *love* a list. I write down everything that needs to be done. Sometimes the list can feel overly full, but it's so satisfying when you can tick things off.

It's ok that some things keep slipping to the bottom of the list, too. For me, it's usually scheduling that overdue dental appointment.

I've learned not to panic if I don't get through everything. Cut yourself some slack, everything will get sorted eventually. If not, well, they're low priority for a reason.

SLOW DOWN

It's so easy to miss the moments that really matter when we're rushing through life. I was going through old photos with my mum recently and I looked at some of them and thought, 'I wish I'd enjoyed that time more.' I just wanted to go back and re-experience the moment and absorb every little detail. It wasn't even big events, like going to Disneyland, that made me the most wistful, but everyday things like going on a walk with Rosie when she was little.

Taking toddlers for a stroll is brilliant because it takes forever just to get to the end of the street, so you have to really take your time and enjoy the experience, and you get to answer all their fantastically tricky and curious questions. I would like to go back and have those moments again, but this time concentrate solely on my daughter without worrying about everything else that I had to do.

We are all time poor and we need to organise and divide our days effectively so we can make time for what's really important, because those moments, particularly with our children, are so precious. When was the last time you sat down and took time out to appreciate what you have? I don't consciously do any kind of mindfulness or meditation – and I know those words sometimes make people recoil in horror – I really just mean taking a moment to do a crossword, read a chapter of a book or watch a soap. We simply don't press the pause button enough. Having some 'me time' is such a joy. Whether you feel like you 'deserve it' or not (you always do), try to take half an hour every day for yourself. Even if some days you can only spare five minutes, taking time to breathe and look around you will make you feel even more capable afterwards.

Ironically, I think mindfulness is something that I do without knowing it. I'm not about to start sitting around chanting while people ding Himalayan singing bowls, but I do try my hardest to concentrate on the positives and appreciate the moment.

During a recent camping trip, Steve and I had to cross the border from Zambia to Botswana by ferry. I started talking to a man in the very long queue who was waiting to take his heavy lorry across. The ferry was tiny so it could only take one big truck and another, smaller, vehicle like our Jeep per crossing. There were many more lorries than cars queuing, so I asked him, 'It's going to be a bit of a wait for you, isn't it, if all these lorries are in front of you?'

He smiled and said, 'Don't worry, I've already been waiting for two weeks.'

He'd slept in his truck for *two weeks* just to do that crossing, and his attitude was, 'it is what it is'. I admired his patience and calm. That man probably has to wait a fortnight every time he does that crossing and he just lets it go. We can learn a lot from people like him.

Can you imagine someone in the UK having to wait that long for a journey? You see people queuing up for a coffee and getting annoyed because they have to wait for two other people to be served first. We can all spare five minutes to chat to someone, or wait to be served in a shop without huffing and puffing.

Lorraine Kelly

FIND YOUR HAPPY PLACE

I'm going to sound so boring now but I find most big, flash celebrity events a bit of an ordeal. It took me a long time to admit that to myself because I always thought I *should* love them. In my opinion, it's just a lot of people standing around making small talk, mostly about themselves. I feel the same about film premieres (although if it's *Star Trek*, I'm there).

I've been to some amazing events over the years and I'm so glad I got to experience them, but I get just as much enjoyment from going for lunch with a friend now.

I've got pals who still go clubbing at weekends and I think that's brilliant. I admire their energy, but I've done all that and I get my dance fix at my exercise class. We're all different and we need to find out what works for us and how we want to spend our days (and nights!).

I like a quiet life. I go to Orkney every year and I would live there in a second. It couldn't be more different to Singapore where my brother and daughter live and work, but both are my happy places. When I'm back in Scotland and it's just me and our dog Angus out in the fresh air, I feel so relaxed. It's like a form of meditation for me, and it's totally free! I don't think you necessarily need to sit for hours on end chanting and ohm-ing to clear your head. I'm sure that works brilliantly for some people, but others find doing the shopping or school run enjoyable, or that cooking the dinner enables them to switch off for a while.

So what makes your head empty a little? For me, climbing to the top of a big hill and admiring the view is heaven, but I can imagine that would be someone's worst nightmare. Working out what you love should be a priority because you can draw on those moments, no matter how small. Sometimes all you need is a long bath and a little bit of time away from the kids.

We sometimes aim too high and don't see what's in front of us. I love a holiday as much as the next person, and I've been lucky enough to have been to some wonderful places, but the place I feel most at peace is anywhere that I'm sitting with Steve, Rosie and Angus and not a word is being said.

Sometimes your happy place is simply about who you are with. My ultimate happy place is on my sofa with a never-ending cup of tea, watching a good box set. The cherry on the cake is if the weather is rubbish, then you don't feel bad about sitting inside and doing nothing!

EXERCISE

Here's my current list of things that make me happy:

1. *An unexpected call from my daughter who just wants a chat, and hearing all her news.*

2. *Finding an episode of* Frasier *I've never seen before.*

3. *Finding jeans that fit perfectly (ditto for summer sandals that are comfy and yet somehow still elegant).*

4. *Finally finding the perfect shade of foundation.*

5. *Sunday morning: cooked breakfast (potato scone with black pudding and a poached egg on top), reading the papers, taking Angus for a walk and looking forward to a roast dinner.*

6. *The smell of a freshly cut lawn.*

7. *Daffodils peeking up shyly through the snow to herald the arrival of spring.*

8. *The satisfaction of clearing out all my cupboards and drawers. The house looks exactly the same but I know that everything is in order.*

9. *Watching the birds in the garden.*

10. *Singing along to my favourite song on the radio, especially if I'm alone and can really let rip and throw in some dubious dance moves.*

Write a list of ten things, people or places that make you happy.

1. _____

2. _____

3. _____

4. _____

5. _____

6. _____

7. _____

8. _____

9. _____

10. _____

ONLINE OVERLOAD

So, you've found your happy place, now enjoy it! Social media is terrible for stealing away the moments you should be spending chilling and relaxing, whether on your own or with the people you love. We are so busy trying to record every second of our lives and broadcast it to everyone we know that we don't enjoy just being in the moment. It drives me mad when I see a couple in a restaurant looking at their phones and ignoring each other. It's even worse when only one person is glued to their mobile – that person is basically saying that looking at Twitter or dancing goats on YouTube is more important than the real person sitting opposite them.

If you can't stop yourself from looking at your phone when you're in company, at least ration it. Have respect for the person you're with. I keep my phone near me because my daughter is in a different time zone and she may need me, and I do have to check it for work, but I will only do that intermittently. Ninety-nine times out of a hundred whatever call, email, or text comes in can wait.

Have nights with your friends where you put your phones away and focus on each other. Make it a rule that you only check them once an hour, if at all, so you give each other your full attention the rest of the time. I interviewed someone who said that if she goes out for dinner or drinks with her friends, the first person who looks at their phone has to pay the bill. I love that. What a great deterrent.

When Steve and I went to Antarctica in 2017, we sailed back from South Georgia to the Falklands. There was a reasonably calm sea for once and the sun was just going down when suddenly some beautiful black-and-white dolphins came out of nowhere, leaping and playing together. I stood for an hour watching them, utterly transfixed. I will never forget that hour because it was as though these amazing creatures were putting on a special show just for me. I didn't need to take a video or photo of them; those images will be in my head forever. If I'd been filming, I wouldn't have been able to fully appreciate the whole experience.

I see this all the time. Parents videoing their school concerts while forgetting to enjoy their child's performance. And what about audience members recording an entire concert by their favourite band on their iPad? Will they ever actually watch the wobbly footage with tinny sound? Just watch the show!

On our Botswanan camping holiday I spent two hours just watching a pride of lions and I've never felt more relaxed. There was no internet or phone signal and nothing to distract me from admiring these incredible animals and watching them interact.

We're suffering from information overload, so it's no wonder our young people are so anxious these days. It used to be that if there was a terrible disaster somewhere you would only find out via a news bulletin or in the paper the following day, but now everything is so instant and we're bombarded with the most horrific images. When I was a child you didn't see images of dead bodies or people shooting each other like you do now It desensitises us, which is dangerous.

Lorraine Kelly

I made a conscious decision to come off Twitter earlier in the year and I feel so much better for it. I felt as if I was being bombarded by negativity 24/7, and I was also getting addicted. Now, I will log on and have a little look every now and again, and repost something if someone is fundraising or saying something, but as a rule I stay away.

I have an Instagram account but I mainly post pictures and videos of my dog Angus. I often get asked where my clothes are from, so I post pictures of my outfit to let people see which high-street store or supermarket they were from.

I sometimes read the comments underneath my posts, and while most are positive, I've also had some cruel reactions from trolls saying, 'You look old, fat and ugly.' I will be honest, it stings, but you can't let it get to you. You just can't. If someone is abusive, I mute them and then they are effectively just ranting into an empty room. You have to think of trolls as ants with megaphones, and maybe even find it in your heart to feel sorry for them.

These days, anyone can message someone they don't know and say vile things. This makes it easy for them to be hurtful, but I still don't understand why someone would think, 'I'm going to abuse someone and make their day really miserable.' I would never wake up of a morning and think, 'Today, I'm going to make someone feel terrible about themselves.' You must be incredibly unhappy to go to the effort of trying to make someone else unhappy. It comes from a bad place of vindictiveness, jealousy and spite.

When I was younger and social media wasn't around, the only way I knew if a member of the public didn't like me was if they sent me a letter, which was usually written in green or purple ink! We also had what was called the Duty Log, a list of all the calls and comments that viewers made about the show while we were on air. Someone might ring in to say they liked the show, but sometimes people would say they didn't like my accent or they couldn't understand me. In my early career, I worried about my accent, so those comments hurt. I suppose it was an early form of trolling, but it was nothing compared to what we have to deal with now. I mean, people even message me to slag off the cushions we have on the sofa. Who has the time?

I can get 100 positive comments, then there will be one that's mean and of course that'll be the one I can't get out of my head. Comments about my clothes or hair don't bother me all that much, but I get distressed if anyone says they don't like an interview I've done, or that I didn't ask the right questions.

The thing is, I'm not daft, and I know when I've done a good job during a show or if there was room for improvement. I don't need someone I've never met to rant at me about it. I am very aware of my own faults, thank you very much. Of course constructive criticism is useful, and I welcome that sort of feedback, but when someone makes it personal, that's just mean; it's not constructive, it's downright nasty.

So if you feel under attack online, try not to read the comments or allow those people's opinions into your head. And you absolutely must not change your behaviour according to what they've said – then they've won, and they do not *deserve* to win. I've decided not to let that negativity into my life; it gives you a skewed idea of the world, it affects your confidence and your well-being, and I don't need it.

It's not just celebrities that suffer bullying. Anyone who is on social media is under scrutiny now. Everyone is a little bit famous in their own way, and people have that direct line to you that never used to exist. Even lovely, decent people get attacked. People troll David Attenborough, for goodness' sake, which should be against the law! I honestly think a brilliant scientist could find a cure for cancer and someone would still find horrible things to say about them.

While part of me feels sorry for trolls, I also want to hunt them down and say, 'What the hell are you doing? Why are you being so mean?' All actions have consequences, and sometimes a person who is being hounded is so utterly devastated that they take their own life. People have died because they couldn't cope with online bullying.

There is also so much attention-seeking on social media. It's dangerous to hinge your self-esteem on how many likes you get for a post. Don't get me wrong, when I look and 60,000 people have liked a video of Angus, I'm chuffed and I hope his antics have brightened their days, but it's not a benchmark of how good I feel about myself. We have to protect our children from becoming too reliant on likes and affirmations from strangers, rather than talking and interacting with friends and family.

Technology isn't going anywhere and it's essential that we keep up with advancements. We can't keep harking back to the so-called 'good old days', because we'll get left behind. Every generation has its battles, and trolls are one of ours.

However, social media can also be a fun, positive and powerful tool, and it can even bring about much-needed change. There have been some hugely important online campaigns that have made a real difference. Personally, though, I would rather spend my time in the real world, because that's what really matters.

EXERCISE

Consider how you might spend less time online. Spend a day without your phone, just to see if you can. Notice what you miss and what you don't. Is your life better if you check Facebook 20 times a day, or do you find you feel calmer without it?

Delete the apps from your phone if checking your social media has become an unconscious habit, and only allow yourself a set time limit on them each day. There are apps, for example, that track how much time you spend on each app, and even block access when you've reached your pre-set limit.

FOOD FOR THOUGHT

I really hope this section has proved helpful and given you plenty to think about. If you've been feeling a bit gloomy, hopefully the advice and exercises will enable you to think more positively and bring back some of your spark!

GLOW

This might be a generalisation, but I believe women put everyone else before themselves. Children come first for those lucky enough to have them, then partners, then pets, then friends, then acquaintances, and then way down at the bottom there we are, gasping for a bit of care or attention for ourselves. This section will help you to look after your body so that you can truly glow.

If we run ourselves ragged or make ourselves ill by not looking after ourselves properly, we're not going to be able to look after anyone else. You need to take care of yourself every bit as much as you do others, otherwise you're no use to anyone.

Listen to what your body is telling you. I always know when I've overdone things because I get mouth ulcers. When they start appearing, that's my body giving me a tap on the shoulder and a heads up that if I don't take my foot off the gas I'm going to be unwell. I've tried to ignore the warning signs in the past, but they always catch up with me. Your body is clever like that.

We give our cars MOTs but not ourselves. We need spring cleans. As my wonderful TV producer and friend Helen Addis says, 'We check our phones, we check what we look like in the mirror, and we check that our house is tidy, but we don't check our own bodies.' That's never more important than when you go through the menopause, which I passionately feel is too often dismissed or hidden away.

So in this section, I'll encourage you to embrace ageing, look after your body and feel comfortable with your style so that you can go out there and glow.

AGEING

I am asked so often about my age, which is strange, because I think about it so little, really. As a child, I thought that anyone older than 25 was old. Past 50? Ancient. But growing older is nothing like I expected. Mostly, it's been a wonderful journey, but the way my menopause changed my life was a complete shock. So let me tell you more about why getting older is no bad thing, and give you a bit of a survival guide for getting through the menopause.

GETTING OLDER IS WONDERFUL!

If I could go back and give my younger self some advice it would be to stress less. Or not stress *at all*! And, unless your doctor has told you to, don't go on a diet. *Do. Not. Do. It.*

I'm honestly having the best time of my life right now. Our culture prizes youth above all else, but people don't take enough time to think about the *benefits* of getting older.

I feel happier in my own skin now than I ever have, and more willing to cut myself a bit of slack and be kinder to myself. I don't understand why we often find it so easy to show kindness towards others but not towards ourselves. What is that about?

I've become better at taking care of myself as time's gone on. I feel more comfortable in my own skin and I've been able to let go of an unobtainable image of perfection.

When you're with a partner, you may not love every single thing about them, and it might drive you mad when they leave the toilet seat up or talk all the way through your favourite TV programme, but you love them so you accept their imperfections. Why not do that for ourselves, too?

Once we start working on showing ourselves unconditional love, our internal critical voice gets quieter and quieter until we stop noticing it. It's not an overnight job, but it's worthwhile.

Keep challenging any unhelpful negative thoughts that slip in, then your self-acceptance will skyrocket and you can't help but glow.

I certainly feel like I'm a better friend and a better wife now, but also that I'm better at my job than I ever have been. I have much more empathy and I've amassed so much knowledge, which I believe makes me a better interviewer. When you get to a certain age, you usually have more confidence because you'll have 'been there, done that'. And if you haven't, there's still plenty of time. I'm starting astronaut training soon, and I certainly didn't think I'd be doing that when I was back in my teens!

It used to be that you had your career or kids, or both, and then you settled down into retirement and that was it. Nowadays we should all be thinking, 'What an amazing exciting opportunity this is', not 'Oh god, I'm getting older and the children have left home so I no longer have a

EXERCISE

The best way to shut up your inner critic is to start being more aware of it. Negative thoughts might come automatically and you might not even notice how hard you're being on yourself. Start really listening to what you're saying to yourself on a day-to-day basis. Each time you find yourself being self-critical, replace that thought with something positive. It almost sounds too easy, but I promise you, it works!

Here are some examples:

Thought: 'My tummy looks bloated in this dress.'
Replace with: 'No one is going to notice my tummy because my boobs look amazing and I'm having a good hair day.'

Thought: 'My spaghetti Bolognese wasn't as good as it usually is tonight. I'll have to try harder next time.'
Replace with: 'How lucky are my family that I make them lovely home-cooked meals?'

purpose'. You'll have more time on your hands, but that shouldn't be scary. Now you can fill it with whatever you're passionate about. There will probably have been moments over the years when you've thought, 'If I had more time I would do that.' Now is that time, even if it's watching every film Bette Davis ever made, or giving your bedroom a lick of paint. You don't have to give up everything and travel the world to try to find yourself. Sometimes you're already there, sitting in your living room feeling contented, you just don't realise it.

When my brother and I left home, my mum joined a book club and went to exercise classes. She now has hobbies that make her feel energised and excited, she's made lots of new pals and her world has opened up in so many ways.

If there isn't a group you want to join, start one! When my friend moved to the seaside there wasn't a walking group in the area so she put up a notice in her local shop to see if anyone was interested. It's got so many members now and they all go to the beach together or meet for coffee.

Volunteering is also great. You could work in a charity shop, or if you've got a car you could offer to give people lifts to and from hospitals or care homes. How good would that feel? It only needs to be a couple of hours a week.

Keeping yourself occupied is not about frantically filling every hour, but don't go to the other extreme and sit in on your bottom every day watching telly. That should be a treat, not your default position.

EXERCISE

Make a list of all the things you wish you had more time for.

If I had all the time in the world, I would . . .

_____

_____

_____

_____

_____

_____

_____

_____

'GOOD FOR YOUR AGE...'

Age really doesn't matter, and there isn't a law that says you should be grown up or 'sorted' by a certain time. I've met some teenagers who are much older than their years, and I've meet people in their 90s who are incredibly young at heart. It's just about maintaining that spring in your step and staying enthusiastic.

Many women get to a certain age and feel invisible, and I think that's really sad. I try to feel vibrant and sexy and sassy and all those things that I should. We're part of a generation that has been taught to look after ourselves, which is a positive thing, but we are bombarded by beauty treatments that promise the earth (I take all of that with a kilo of salt), and that puts a lot of pressure on all of us. It's one thing to look after your skin, but some treatments cost as much as a family holiday!

We have more older role models than ever now, which is brilliant, but we always hold up the same women, like Joan Collins, Helen Mirren and Meryl Streep. They are indeed all powerhouses, but we need even more women to talk about the benefits of getting older and not just about looking younger or 'good for your age'.

Ageing shouldn't be scary. It broke my heart when I heard that Sherrie Hewson wanted to have another facelift. Any decent man would be lucky to have Sherrie on his arm, and any woman would be lucky to have her as a friend, yet she feels that she's unattractive and more surgery is the answer. Having said that, if it truly makes her feel better then that's her choice, but these operations are only temporary. Instead, Sherrie could build up her inner confidence. She's so lovely as she is, but she doesn't realise it.

Forget a Chanel handbag, the best accessory a woman can have is inner confidence, which shines above all else. I've known girls who can walk into a room and every pair of eyes will be on them. They may not be the most traditionally beautiful woman in that room, but they will have a unique quality, like the ability to make people laugh, and that's what makes them so attractive.

We now see women getting surgery younger and younger. Of course we want to look the best we can be, but a 19-year-old does not need Botox. We've seen so many women who have ruined their faces with filler.

I think I look fine as I am and I will never go under the knife. I like my laughter lines (a much nicer way of saying wrinkles) and I hate to think that women make themselves miserable every time they look in the mirror because of a few extra lines. Unless you do have surgery they're not going away, so why not embrace them? They tell your story. If you do want work done, it's an individual choice, but I wish we could all be more accepting of ourselves and the ageing process, because it's going to happen whether we like it or not.

The Kardashian body type is not realistic. Nothing about the women in that family is normal. Reality TV can sometimes offer a bit of escapist fun, but so many girls think that the way the LA rich and famous live and look is the only measure of success. Having your lips plumped up like a puffer fish isn't considered a bizarre thing to do anymore, which is strange in itself.

Look, if you have a nose that bothers you and you want to do something about it, I get that, but young girls having Botox and fillers put in their youthful faces is terrifying. If this trend continues, thousands of young women (and men) will end up looking exactly the same: as though they're stuck in a wind tunnel with their lips stung by a swarm of bees. Let's be honest, when you see some of the girls who have had a lot of work done without their make-up on, the illusion crumbles. I've seen people who have had so much surgery they look like Klingons.

I hope it's just a trend. In the '60s everyone plucked their eyebrows off, and now big bushy ones are in fashion. I like to think at some point people will stop believing that having gigantic fake lips and enormous bottom implants are desirable.

I'm flattered when someone says I don't look 60, but I don't think we should be defined by a number. You're only as old as you let yourself feel. What does dressing like a 60-year-old mean? When I was a kid it meant a tight grey perm and a shapeless coat, but nowadays 60 is still young.

I absolutely feel like some of my best years are in front of me and I'm excited about what my future holds, and you should be too. Think of all the amazing things you've still got to discover. There are books to be read, holidays to go on and new people to meet. The world is a constant source of wonder.

good things are coming!

WE NEED TO TALK ABOUT THE MENOPAUSE

I'm so relieved that the menopause has been dragged kicking and screaming into the light, because it needs to be spoken about more. So many women suffer in silence, and as much as I loved the incredible reaction we got when we started to discuss it openly on the show last year, it was upsetting to hear just how many women out there are suffering mentally and physically. Discussing the menopause on the show opened the floodgates and it helped so many women (and men). I'm so glad we helped to break down that barrier.

I must admit, I was surprised at the number of high-profile women we approached to come on the show and talk about it who said no because they didn't want to appear old or past it. It's going to happen to us all and let's not forget that some women go through the menopause when they are young or have it triggered by medical treatment. It shouldn't be this big taboo; a woman's worth should no longer be based on her fertility.

Carol Vorderman, Ulrika Jonsson and Meg Mathews generously all spoke about their menopause experiences. Their honesty and me talking about my own experience started a dialogue and gave women permission to be more open and talk to their partners or their friends about how they were feeling. Judging by the feedback, it also helped others to identify with

other women going through the same struggles and realise it wasn't just them feeling that way, which made them feel less alone. I wish more people in the public eye would talk about the menopause as it really makes a difference.

The menopause should be seen as an empowering and positive development in a woman's life. I think post-menopausal woman are in their prime. If you have kids, they'll probably be grown up now, giving you the option to change your life completely if you so desire. It's a time for experimenting and mixing things up. Organise a girls' night out with your pals, dance around the kitchen to cheesy pop songs, or go into a shop and try on something you'd normally never dare wear.

The 'M word' will happen to all women at some point in their lives, yet there's still so much shame around it. We're not taught about it at school, and many GPs are ill-informed. If your GP tries to fob you off with anti-depressants and sleeping tablets, ask for a second opinion. If you're still not getting the care you need, try another practice. Sadly, women's healthcare is often not taken seriously and we have to be our own healthcare advocates. Most of the time we have to do the research for ourselves.

When I went through the menopause I couldn't understand what was happening to me. As I explained earlier, a terrible anxiety hit me like a wave and I felt totally overwhelmed. I lost myself for a while and I felt upset and frustrated, but I still had to go into work each day and paint on a smile. Millions of women share this experience every single day, whether we're going to work, picking the kids or grandkids up from school or caring for other people, and we're just expected to get on with it.

I thought the menopause might be on its way because my periods were dwindling, and then I'd get an especially painful and heavy one, but I wasn't aware of the massive impact it also has on your emotions. Before I went to my GP, I spoke to Dr Hilary Jones and explained how I was feeling. The first thing he said to me was, 'It's hormonal. Of course it is!' Just hearing those words made me feel better because I felt I might finally have some answers and be able to do something about it.

I spoke to my GP about my options and I decided to go on Hormone Replacement Therapy (HRT). The hormones took a couple of months to properly kick in, but once they did it was miraculous. I cannot explain how good it felt to start enjoying everyday things again, and I didn't look back. Your hormones shift all the time, so two years down the line I had to change my prescription, but I felt so reassured knowing that I could read the signs and get the help I needed.

Hormones are incredibly powerful; whether we're hormonal teenagers or dealing with post-natal depression, our bodies and minds are governed by our hormones. Yet, we can be ruled by them and still not know enough about them.

Everyone's menopause is different. Some of us have a nightmare of a time, while others sail through it all serenely without much trouble at all. When I asked my mum about hers she said she couldn't really remember it, which is remarkable – most people I know have struggled in one way or another.

Do whatever you need to do in order to make the whole

experience as painless as possible. HRT worked for me, but I'm not saying it's for everyone and you must be aware of all the facts. There are other treatments and things you can do, such as dietary changes and exercising, but you've got to know about them. I don't think Dr Google is a great place to start, though, because you can end up terrifying the life out of yourself. If you don't feel you're getting the help you need from your GP, ask to be referred to a specialist.

However you decide to tackle your menopause, just please, please don't be embarrassed about it. Half the world's population will go through it, so it's lunacy that we still brush the subject under the carpet.

WE NEED TO TALK ABOUT HORMONES

Dr Louise Newson is evangelical about hormones, and that's why I was so keen to include a comprehensive interview with her in this book. Her help and advice genuinely changed my life for the better. We only really touch on the basics in this interview, so if you want to know more, her book, *Menopause: All you need to know in one concise manual*, is a brilliant guide. Like me, Dr Louise wants to help women and get them talking more about the menopause. With the right help and support, the menopause doesn't have to be a struggle.

First things first, Dr Louise, what exactly are hormones?

Hormones are basically chemical messengers that are produced by various organs in our body, which travel through our bloodstream. We have hormones such as adrenaline (our fight and flight hormone), thyroxine (the hormone which regulates metabolism) and cortisol (our stress hormone), and then we also have our sex hormones, which are produced mainly by our ovaries and include oestrogen, progesterone and even testosterone. Our sex hormones have vital effects on our reproductive system. Cells throughout our body respond to these sex hormones – from our joints to our bones to our brains. You name it, they get everywhere.

What effect do these have on us during the menopause?

Well, we should actually start with the perimenopause, which is the time just before the menopause occurs. At this point some women can start to experience menopausal symptoms. So even though you're not 'officially' menopausal until a year after your last period, change starts many years before your periods stop.

Lots of women experience symptoms while they are still having periods, and so don't realise that they are caused by changing hormones. Symptoms vary a lot, and as they often occur around the time when we're busy with children, work and looking after our parents, we can put them down to working too hard or being worn out.

When does the perimenopause and menopause start?

In the UK, the average age for menopause is 51; 45 for the perimenopause. However, it can be much earlier; around 1 in 100 women under 40 experience an early menopause.

What are the main symptoms of menopause?

Symptoms can change with time and vary between women, but often they include low mood, anxiety, irritability, worsening headaches, migraines, joint pains, muscle aches, fatigue, poor sleep, reduced libido and urinary symptoms.

For some women it begins with hot flushes and night sweats and then with time they develop anxiety. In later years they might experience vaginal dryness, too. There's a whole spectrum of symptoms and women do not usually experience all of them at the same time (unless they are really unlucky), and they can even change month by month.

Some women don't experience any symptoms until they are menopausal or post-menopausal (i.e. when their periods have fully stopped), but for many women, symptoms begin during the perimenopause and continue for many years, even decades.

Everyone assumes that blood tests are usually the first port of call for diagnosing the menopause.

They do, and that can cause a lot of confusion. Hormone levels change and fluctuate all the time. You could have a blood test on five different days and have five different results. Abnormal hormone tests can be useful, but if the results are considered to be 'normal' then women will often be told that their symptoms are unrelated to their hormones, which is often not true.

If you are over 45, your doctor should not need a hormone blood test to diagnose your menopause or perimenopause, the diagnosis can be made on symptoms alone. We use a menopause questionnaire on all our patients in my clinic which includes questions about physical, psychological and vasomotor symptoms, which include hot flushes and night sweats. Women between 40 and 45 years old can sometimes have hormone levels checked to make a diagnosis. Women under 40 years old should have their levels checked at least twice to make the correct diagnosis.

So why do doctors still do blood tests?

We often undertake blood tests in my clinic to exclude other causes for a woman's symptoms, and also to monitor treatment with HRT. For example, we undertake thyroid function tests to ensure a woman's symptoms are not due to an underactive thyroid gland. Thyroid disorders can develop in women around middle age.

Do you have to take other medications into account when taking HRT?

We usually prescribe what is known as 'body identical HRT' and the oestrogen is given as a patch or gel. 'Body identical HRT' simply replaces the hormones that have reduced during the perimenopause or menopause. This method is very safe and does not usually interact with any other medications. There are some types of HRT available on prescription which are not body identical. These usually contain older types of progestogens which can still be effective. They can lead to more side effects in some women compared to the body identical hormones.

Why are many women so afraid of HRT?

In 2002, the results of a large American study called the Women's Health Initiative were published. The results were leaked to the press before the results were properly analysed. The reports stated that women taking HRT had a greater risk of breast cancer and heart disease which understandably led to women and healthcare professionals being concerned about HRT. In this study, though, the average age of women was 64, an age when women have already gone through the menopause. In addition, many women in this study were overweight or obese and many had experienced heart attacks in the past. They were all given an older type of HRT which contained oestrogen, taken in tablet form and an older type of progestogen (neither of these were body identical hormones). This type of HRT is associated with increased risk of heart disease, clots and a small risk of breast cancer, so we usually no longer prescribe it.

The results of this study were then analysed properly and the results showed that the increased risk of breast cancer and heart disease was actually likely to be due to other risk factors and not due to HRT. These women have now been studied for 14 years and the results have shown that those women who continued to take HRT had a lower future risk of conditions such as heart disease and osteoporosis, and also a lower risk of death from all causes, including from cancer.

Since this study was undertaken there have been numerous other studies that have shown how safe and effective HRT is. Taking body identical HRT (oestrogen with micronised progesterone) is associated with a lower future risk of heart disease, osteoporosis, osteoarthritis, type 2 diabetes and also dementia.

So it's really important to look at the bigger picture of why a woman is taking HRT. Taking the right dose and type of HRT will improve both a woman's symptoms and her future health, due to lowering future risk of various diseases.

What about the claims that women put on weight when they go on HRT?

Actually, it's often the opposite. Metabolic changes that occur in the body during the perimenopause and menopause often result in women putting on weight, especially across their middles, which often improves when they are taking the right dose and type of HRT. Once women start taking HRT and feel better they often lose weight because their energy levels improve, they are more interested in healthy eating and they are no longer comfort eating or drinking excess alcohol to numb their symptoms.

We know that women who are overweight, do not exercise and who drink excess alcohol have an increased future risk of breast cancer, so taking HRT can help women live a more healthy lifestyle and reduce risk factors.

What about the risk of blood clots that we often hear about?

Oestrogen patches or gels eliminate the risk of clots because the hormone goes directly into the bloodstream and it bypasses the liver, which produces our clotting factors.

What about people who say 'well, we managed without HRT in the old days'?

Replacing hormones with HRT is similar to the way that we give thyroxine to a person with hypothyroidism, or give insulin to a person with diabetes.

Back in Victorian times, the average age of menopause was around 57, and we died at around 59, so the condition was less relevant than it is now. Nowadays, the average age for menopause is 51 and life expectancy is far older, usually in the 80s, which means that many women are living for decades with low levels of hormones in their bodies.

There is still a large amount of stigma around HRT, which is disappointing and often leads to unnecessary confusion. When I first told some friends I was taking HRT, many said, 'That makes you sound really old.' It's so negative! Someone even told me taking HRT was simply a 'fad' that will change in a few years. However, we have excellent and long-standing research that clearly demonstrates the numerous health benefits of taking HRT.

Women read negative publicity about HRT and think 'I'm not taking that'. It's so sad because the vast majority of the women we see in my clinic are struggling with their symptoms and quality of their lives. Some women are very low in their moods and even suicidal. Many women we talk to have had to give up their jobs due to symptoms such as anxiety, memory problems and fatigue. Women often tell us that they are falling asleep on the sofa every afternoon because they are so tired, yet they can't sleep at night.

What are the alternatives to HRT?

There are alternative medications that your doctor can prescribe for some symptoms. Certain types of antidepressants may improve hot flushes in some women, even those who are not depressed. However, use of such medications can be limited as they can have side-effects such as nausea, worsened libido or insomnia.

There are thousands of alternative products available from shops or over the internet that are marketed for helping with menopausal symptoms, including red clover, black cohosh and St John's wort. However, there's very limited research or evidence to support their effectiveness and some are associated with significant health risks, especially if you have a history of breast cancer or are taking other prescribed medications, as there may be interactions.

I have seen women who have spent small fortunes on alternative preparations, but herbal doesn't automatically mean it's safe. Many herbal medicines have unpredictable doses and purity. If you do choose to explore herbal medicine as a treatment option, it would be best to consult with a qualified medical herbalist: www.nimh.org.uk/find-a-herbalist/

Although there is little scientific evidence to support their use in alleviating menopausal symptoms, some women use acupuncture or magnet therapy with some success.

Others find drinking certain herbal teas can lead to a better night's sleep and a feeling of wellbeing, while some find that aromatherapy oils help to relax and improve symptoms of anxiety or depression; lavender may help with poor sleep. Therapies such as aromatherapy, mindfulness, CBT or yoga, which allow you to relax and focus on yourself, can help you cope better with menopausal symptoms, while stopping smoking, taking regular exercise, losing weight and cutting down on alcohol consumption have been shown to improve symptoms such as hot flushes and night sweats. These lifestyle measures are also beneficial for our future health and wellbeing.

Why does the menopause affect sleep?

Many women wake up during the night because of night sweats, and others find they simply wake at various times and are then unable to go back to sleep. Our hormones oestrogen and testosterone can be really important for our sleep so when levels of these hormones reduce then our sleep can be negatively affected.

In addition, sometimes anxiety caused by a hormone imbalance can prevent good-quality sleep, and being tired can have a detrimental effect on health.

So many perimenopausal and menopausal women are incorrectly being given antidepressants and sleeping tablets to cope with their low moods and sleep problems. I did a survey recently of nearly 3,000 women, of which 66 per cent had been given antidepressants instead of HRT.

Some women breeze through their menopause whereas others really suffer. Why is that?

Some women do suffer more than others, but even if you do sail through it, once your periods stop, your low hormone levels still increase the risk of diabetes, osteoporosis, heart disease, arthritis and dementia.

Women who have suffered from PMS or postnatal depression often have a worse time with the psychological symptoms of menopause because these women are very sensitive to changing hormone levels in their brains. These women often stop socialising and they tell me that they spend days alone at home not wanting to see anyone. Some women experience irrational anxiety or stop driving because they feel panic-stricken. Other psychological symptoms such a low mood, mood swings, reduced motivation and irritability can be common, too.

Can HRT help with PMS?

Quite often women who have terrible PMS will respond well to having oestrogen a week or so before their period when oestrogen levels drop. This tops up the hormone levels, so women can feel much better.

Are there different types of HRT?

HRT is not a one-size-fits-all, there are many different types and doses. Oestrogen is the most important hormone and this is usually given through the skin as a patch or gel. Unless a woman has had a hysterectomy, she needs to take a progestogen, either through an oral capsule, tablet or the Mirena coil. Some women also benefit from testosterone, which can improve libido, mood, energy and motivation.

Why is it so difficult for women to receive help with their menopause?

It can sometimes be hard to diagnose as there are so many symptoms related to the perimenopause and menopause. Many healthcare professionals have received very little training about the menopause, which urgently needs to change. Many women take expensive hormones from private clinics because they wrongly think they need to take bespoke treatment, but it is important that women receive regulated hormones that are safe.

I am not saying that every woman needs to take HRT, as it's a personal and individual choice. However, a large number of women across the world are still denied HRT when they would benefit from taking it, which is very sad and frustrating. I see many women in my clinic who have been wrongly told that they cannot have HRT as it is 'dangerous' or 'risks clots'. Some women are even falsely told that they are too young to take HRT. It is essential that women are given evidence-based and non-biased information.

We often recommend women try taking HRT for a few months and then review how they feel. Many women do not realise how many symptoms they have been experiencing until they feel better through taking HRT.

How important is diet when it comes to hormones?

Diet is very important for all of us, and especially during the menopause. Eating a healthy, balanced Mediterranean-style diet is beneficial for overall good health.

Many women notice that when their hormone levels reduce they experience carbohydrate cravings and really want to eat sugar.

Many metabolic changes occur in our bodies due to our changing hormone levels. Often women put on weight around their midline because their bodies try to conserve fat. A small amount of oestrogen is produced from fat cells, so this weight gain occurs as the body has a last-ditch attempt to cling on to oestrogen.

Sometimes women no longer have the motivation to cook properly and they also find that they are comfort eating more. It becomes a vicious cycle and even if women are only putting on a little bit of weight each year, this weight gain can add up to a lot over ten years or so.

So which foods should we avoid?

Some people find certain diets or foods exacerbate their symptoms. Hot spicy foods and caffeine can often make hot flushes worse, while refined sugar causes lots of problems. The metabolic changes that occur during the perimenopause and menopause often result in women having more insulin (a hormone that affects our blood sugar levels) resistance.

If you eat a bar of chocolate you will feel great for a few minutes as your glucose levels quickly increase, then your insulin level will follow suit to cope with the glucose. Your glucose levels will drop back down quickly so that half an hour later you will feel hungry again. If you eat less sugary food your blood sugar level will increase slowly, as will your insulin level before it plateaus, meaning you'll feel full for the next two or three hours. That's obviously much better for our bodies because we are not driving our pancreas to flood out insulin in these spurts. When that happens over time the pancreas can become 'tired' and you're more likely to develop diabetes.

How important is exercise for treating hormone issues?

Exercising produces endorphins, which can have a positive effect on our minds as well as our bodies. Many menopausal women find they feel demotivated and flat. They can also experience joint pains and muscle stiffness because oestrogen is an anti-inflammatory.

Hormones are also important for muscle strength. Many women tell me that their stamina is reduced and their muscles are weaker so they can't do as much exercise as they used to. They often give up exercising altogether, which clearly can be detrimental for future health. HRT can make all the difference to their stamina and ability to exercise.

Does the menopause cause facial hair?

Facial hair is often caused by an imbalance between oestrogen and testosterone, because often oestrogen declines more quickly relative to testosterone. Some women will still get facial hair even when their hormones are balanced, as this is unrelated to their hormones.

Why can skin also suffer during the menopause?

Some women find their skin becomes very dry and itchy and isn't as glowing as it used to be. Oestrogen is important for building collagen in the skin and it can help reduce moisture loss from the skin, too. Often women find that when they take HRT their skin texture improves and becomes less dry. It also reduces fine lines and wrinkles by plumping the skin! HRT helps to improve the blood supply to the skin, too.

Are supplements helpful for hormonal imbalances?

There are a huge amount of very expensive supplements marketed for perimenopausal and menopausal women, which concerns me. People generally think more expensive supplements are better, but sadly this isn't always true.

Some supplements may help reduce symptoms such as hot flushes, but these are not going to help strengthen bones or reduce future risk of heart disease. The government recommend that everyone take vitamin D, because this is the sunlight vitamin that we usually do not get enough of. Some women take a good-quality magnesium supplement, and I personally think people should take a good-quality fish oil that contains EPA and DHA; these are really important types of omega 3 which help to reduce inflammation and can also reduce future risk of heart disease. I also often recommend people take a good-quality probiotic, because optimal gut health can improve serotonin levels, which can help to improve our moods.

BODY

We only get one body, and we want it to support us for as long as possible. That means putting good things in, taking time out to heal it and treating ourselves as well as we possibly can.

LOOK AFTER YOUR BODY AND IT WILL LOOK AFTER YOU

Like most people, I have a busy lifestyle which means holidays are precious. I don't mean having a long weekend away once in a blue moon, I mean taking proper time out from everything. Even if you're just spending the time at home relaxing, it will help. Studies have shown that time away from work reduces stress and stress-related aches and pains, like headaches and backaches. Having a break also makes us more productive in the long run and helps to improve our sleep.

Happily, life expectancy has increased, which means that 60 is the new 50, or even 40. However, that doesn't mean we can be complacent. It's our duty to look after ourselves. If you notice that something is wrong, or even just different, with your body, go to the doctor. Don't sit and suffer in silence, and don't be fobbed off. It can be hard when you want to get a second opinion because you feel like you're cheating on your doctor, but they're professionals, so don't feel bad. Your wellbeing is far more important than a bit of awkwardness or embarrassment.

This extended life expectancy has created a 'sandwich generation' of people who are caring for both their children and their parents, which can be an incredible strain. If parents become frail or unwell it often seems to fall to daughters to provide care. When we're taking care of everyone else, our own health often falls way down the priority list. Your health is even more important when you have other people to look after.

If you feel like everyone wants a little piece of you and you have nothing left to give, that's when you'll become run down and no use to anyone!

EXERCISE

Think about what warning signs your body gives when you're run down. What actions could you take when they appear, to prevent full-on exhaustion?

Warning signs:

_____

_____

_____

_____

_____

_____

_____

Actions:

_____

_____

_____

_____

_____

_____

_____

ALTERNATIVE HEALTHCARE

I am very open-minded about natural, alternative healthcare. As much as I rely on science because I'm practical, I've seen too many things happen over the years to not say 'there is another way'.

However, some alternative therapies are a bit 'out there' and I'm not sure they're for me, and I do think it is important to be wary of practitioners and do your research before undergoing any new treatment. There was the case, for example, of a woman who claimed she lived only on fresh air and sunshine. Sadly, some vulnerable people followed her example and became very ill as a result.

If you are keen to explore alternative therapies, here are some helpful guidelines:

- *Always make your GP the first port of call if you have a pre-existing health problem or if you're pregnant. Some alternative therapies can interact with medications, so be sure to check that they will be ok for you.*

- *Osteopathy and chiropractice are the only two alternative treatments that are regulated by law and must stick to certain codes of practice. Aside from those, alternative practitioners aren't regulated, meaning it's legal for therapists to practise without any formal training or previous experience, so proper research is essential.*

- *The Complementary and Natural Healthcare Council independently regulate therapists (www.cnhc.org.uk). You can quickly and easily enter a therapist's details on the website to check if they're registered.*

- *If you feel at all worried about going to see someone new, take along a friend or family member to your first appointment.*

I do believe in 'whatever gets you through', and I would never judge anyone for trying something new. We're all different and what doesn't work for one person might work for another. I tried acupuncture in my 20s when I had a terrible back problem and it made such a difference. It was still considered to be pretty experimental in those days, but it really worked for me.

My friend Joyce and I had some reiki right after we ran the New York marathon. Practitioners were offering their services for free and by that point we were so exhausted even my hair was aching, so I would have tried anything. I really did feel it was beneficial.

Another time when I was staying in Thailand with my brother we both had reflexology. The old fella who was doing my brother's feet kept looking really confused. It turns out he was trying to find my brother's spleen on the usual reflexology point, but he couldn't; Graham had his spleen removed when he was a kid due to an accident. There's no way the reflexologist could have known that, and it made me think that maybe there is something to it.

Feeling tired is the curse of anyone that works shifts or has young kids, and definitely for people who work in breakfast TV.

I've had times where I'm lying in bed at night worrying about a big interview I've got to do the following day and I'll be going over and over things in my head and trying to make sure I haven't forgotten anything. Then other thoughts will start to creep in and before I know it two hours will have passed and I start to panic about not getting enough sleep.

I haven't slept for eight hours for years – I generally sleep for about five or six hours a night. I usually get to bed at around 10 or 11pm and I get up at 4.30am. People often assume I nap in the afternoon because I get up so early, but I find it really hard to do that and I would rather just soldier on to bedtime. On the rare occasion when I do fall asleep in the middle of the day, I always wake up feeling really groggy and it takes ages for me to clear my head, so I avoid it. I know that for some people napping is wonderful, and lots of experts highly recommend it, but I just can't do it!

Working to improve your sleep is one of the best things you can do for your mental and emotional health. Being stressed can make you feel overtired, and if, like me, you don't have the time or can't have a siesta, just taking little moments out of your day to stay calm and recharge is essential, even if it's only standing still and breathing deeply for 30 seconds.

If you really are exhausted all the time, get yourself checked out, because it could be for other reasons than an over-active brain and not being able to switch off. It's always best to get a medical opinion if you're in any way worried.

The one rule that made all the difference in the world to my quality of sleep was banishing my phone and iPad from the bedroom. If you have your devices in your room, there's always the temptation to check the news and Instagram, and before you know it you've disappeared down an internet rabbit hole. It's so easy to Google one little thing and still be there an hour and a half later reading about something completely different. Or there could be one thing on Facebook or Twitter that annoys you and keeps you awake for hours on end as it circles your head.

I use an old-fashioned alarm clock so I don't rely on my phone to wake me up. Rosie knows she can call the landline if she really needs to get hold of me during the night. Due to the time difference in Singapore, she is up and at her work while we are sleeping.

I always have a notepad next to my bed where I write down things that are bothering me, as a way to get them out of my head but also to rationalise my worries. It may be that once you've written down what's worrying you, you can come up with a solution, or you realise it's not something that you can change right now so there's no point fretting. Something that has kept you awake all night often seems ridiculous in the cold light of day.

I also keep a book by my bed that I know inside out. It's about Shackleton's journey to Antarctica and I almost know it word for word, so reading it soothes me.

Other good sleep tips I've been given over the years are:

- *Drink more water throughout the day. Being dehydrated makes you exhausted, so it's worth making sure you are taking in enough water. Cut down on caffeinated tea and coffee throughout the day, too.*

- *Avoid sugary foods to regulate your energy levels.*

- *Check your vitamin levels. Poor sleep can be a sign of vitamin D deficiency.*

- *Exercise regularly.*

- *Make sure you can't see the clock from your bed. There's nothing worse than thinking 'Only five hours until I have to get up', and then, 'Now it's four and a half. I'm going to be knackered!'*

- *Stay away from technology altogether! Sleep expert Dr Rangan Chatterjee recommends a 'no-tech 90', which means no technology (including TV) for 90 minutes before bed.*

- *Do some meditation or deep breathing before sleep. There are some great apps, such as Calm, to guide you through this.*

- *Put a few drops of lavender oil on your pillow.*

- *Avoid alcohol. Drinking booze may help to knock you out, but the sleep you have will be of poor quality.*

- *Drink a mug of chamomile or sleep tea half an hour before bed.*

- *It sounds so obvious, but make sure your mattress is comfy and your room temperature is right.*

- *Make your bedroom a place you love so that you look forward to going to bed – wash your bedding regularly, treat yourself to some plump new pillows or a cosy hot water bottle for winter nights.*

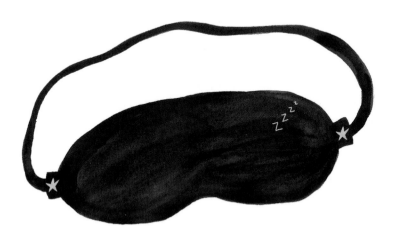

THE 'F' WORD

I hate the word 'fat' and I think it should be banned. So much fear and emotion is tied up in those three little letters. It's a word that followed me around my whole life, until the day I decided it would no longer feature in my vocabulary.

I've done every stupid diet in the world and I must have gained and lost the equivalent of my own body weight 10 times over the years. I first started worrying about my figure when I was in my mid-teens and I realised that, like all the women in our family, I didn't have a flat tummy. From then on, I was determined to diet it away. What a waste of time and energy.

My friends and I always used to talk about what diets we were on at school and compare notes and hunger pangs. Whether it was the grapefruit diet (utterly ridiculous), the boiled egg diet (great if you want chronic constipation) or the cabbage soup diet (wonderful if you want to clear the room with a fart), we would be obsessed with it for a few days, get frustrated when we didn't instantly turn into Twiggy, then go back to eating crisps again. I love my grub and I always have. When I look back at that teenager who thought she was fat I want to go back in time and tell her she was gorgeous.

I joined my first slimming club when I was just 16, and I felt amazing when I lost 10 pounds in a relatively short time, which wasn't hard when I was eating an apple for breakfast, nothing for lunch and then picking at my dinner. Needless to say, as soon as I started eating three meals a day plus snacks again, that

10 pounds went straight back on, and so began many years of soul-destroying yo-yo dieting.

When I first became a TV reporter I had to grab whatever I could when I was on the go, which meant I had a lot of take-aways and petrol-station pies, so my weight crept up and up. Every now and again I'd find the willpower to cut out the junk food and I'd lose half a stone and then . . . well, you know the outcome.

I was always hopping on and off the scales, and the number on that dial would affect my entire day. If I'd lost weight I'd feel great and I'd give myself a pat on the back, but if I'd put on weight I would feel miserable and want to reach for the nearest bun. There were times I'd look in the mirror and feel good, and there were times when I felt totally dejected, and it was all governed by how big or small I felt.

I'd go to a diet club on a Monday night after I'd eaten like a piglet all weekend. I'd starve myself all day and then be upset and annoyed that I hadn't lost any weight. I'd feel so disappointed I'd go for a fish-and-chip supper afterwards. It was such a horrible, self-destructive pattern.

Really, it's not rocket science. If you eat too much, especially when it's mainly junk food and you don't do any exercise, you are going to put on weight. But I was in denial for so long and thought there must be an easy way that worked. I just had to find it! I couldn't have been more wrong.

Luckily, I didn't ever have an eating disorder, but I can see how people go to extremes when they're in a state of panic and want a quick fix. It can spiral into something very dangerous, and

I know from speaking to a lot of women and men who have suffered from eating disorders over the years that once you are in its grip, it won't let go of you. Eating disorders affect so many people; I've noticed sufferers are often intelligent, driven and very hard on themselves. Professional help is vital for their recovery.

Food can be an addiction for some people. Go and talk to your doctor or ask to be referred if you have a tendency to binge or you feel that your eating is out of control. If you have serious issues around food no amount of dieting is going to work, and there is professional support available.

Naturally, I put on weight when I was pregnant with Rosie, and a year after I had her people were still asking me when she was due because the baby weight hadn't shifted. I went up to a size 16. In fact, 16s were tight, but I didn't want to admit to myself that I was an 18.

I knew it was a slippery slope and I could easily have ended up obese. Despite what we're conditioned to believe, it is possible to be a size 18 and healthy, but after a doctor told me I was endangering my health I made a real effort to eat properly and exercise, but it took a long time for me to achieve balance.

Ever since I gave up dieting, my body has evened out. I refuse to go on a diet ever again. I no longer count grams of fat or calories and I have learned the hard way that daft diets ultimately make you fat. Now I know that it's all about a healthy eating plan (one that allows you to fall off the wagon now and again, as we are all only human) combined with exercise you enjoy.

I eat a balanced diet with plenty of fruit and vegetables and

protein and I listen to what my body is telling me. If I'm hungry, I eat, and if I'm not, I don't eat for the sake of it. That's it – that's the miracle cure! I've realised that you don't have to live on mung beans and quinoa to be healthy, or starve yourself to be slim.

I do let myself go sometimes, and that's all right. If I go away for a weekend I will eat what I want and enjoy myself, but I make sure I don't get into a 'sod it' pattern and carry on eating chips or cake all the following week. If you eat a giant pizza three times a day, every day, you're going to have to really fight to keep the weight off, but it's fine to have one now and again as a treat. Moderation is key.

The reason why there are so many faddy diets is because they don't work. Even if you do lose weight, when you go back to your old way of eating the pounds pile back on again. Diets are not sustainable. No one can survive on three diet shakes a day for the rest of their life.

I know one woman who didn't realise she liked salad until she was in her 40s. She only ever ate salad if she was trying to lose weight, so she viewed it negatively, as a kind of punishment food. Now she chooses to eat it because she really enjoys it. She's realised that salad isn't just limp lettuce leaves and a few sad cucumber slices, it's about experimenting with lovely fresh foods and delicious ingredients. A good salad is so tasty.

I do tend to eat sensibly during the week but I certainly don't exist on sticks of celery, because I'd be miserable. I eat a balanced diet and I'm no longer afraid of food. Once you fear food it has power over you, but when you realise that eating one take-away doesn't mean you're going to wake up a stone heavier the following day, you can begin to relax and get on with the important job of enjoying those treats without feeling like a terrible person.

I do think as mothers, grandmothers, sisters and aunties we have a responsibility not to talk about diets in front of children, boys included. If your child sees you on the scales constantly or hears you asking 'Does my bum look big in this?' they are obviously going to pick up on your preoccupation with your body. They will believe this is normal behaviour, and then they will copy it. We don't want our children to think that food is the enemy; it should nourish us and make us feel better, not scare us.

It's ridiculous that we say, 'I've been good today' or 'I've been bad today'. What do you mean, you've been good? You haven't rescued a kitten from a tree, you've just said no to having cake. Eating a KitKat with a cup of tea does not make you an awful person.

I tried not to make food a big issue when Rosie was growing up. I would give her little plates of fruit that she could snack on and we encouraged her to try lots of different foods. We've been lucky enough to travel a lot, even when she was tiny, so she's tried food from all over the world, including Japan, Africa and the USA. She grew up with a healthy attitude towards food and she's always sending me photos of the amazing grub she enjoys in Singapore and while travelling in South East Asia. She also does yoga and enjoys walking, cycling and hiking, but she still loves a cheeky cocktail.

We all need to reach a point where we are comfortable with our bodies. If you are supposed to be a size 14 and that's your natural shape, please don't spend the rest of your life starving yourself because you want to be a size 10. Your body will naturally find its way back to its happy weight at some point, and then you'll end up starting the fight all over again. I've been there and, believe me, it's relentless and it doesn't work.

So many of us battle against our bodies and try to be something we're not, and it's exhausting. Some people are just naturally teeny tiny and that's fine. Stacey Dooley is a slip of a thing and you can tell that's her natural shape. Then you look at Nesh, who is one of the models on my show, she's a perfectly proportioned size 16. Genetically, she is supposed to be that size, and she is *beautiful*.

I fought against my natural shape for so many years. Now, I no longer own scales and I couldn't tell you exactly how much I weigh, and that's liberating. I'm between a size 10 and a 12 and that's fine with me. If my jeans start feeling a bit tight, I know I've been eating too much and not exercising enough, but I don't let it stress me out. I just go for a longer walk and cut out some treats for a bit.

So don't make yourself miserable by going on a stupid starvation diet to become a size zero. Practise balance, and find where your body wants to be so you don't spend the next 20, 30 or 40 years losing and gaining weight in a horrible circle of despair.

We're set up for failure when it comes to our bodies. We're brainwashed from a young age that being thin brings happiness, as if being a size 8 means you'll leap out of bed and dance joyfully all the way to work because life is so amazing when you're slim. If there's one thing I know not to be true, it's the idea that 'if I lose a stone everything will be great'. It won't. Your life will still be the same and you'll continue to have the same problems, you'll just be buying smaller knickers.

If you look at a dress and think, 'If I lose a stone that dress will look great on me and everything will be gorgeous in my life', stop. You are already gorgeous. A few pounds, or even a few stones, do not dictate whether someone is good enough. You are good enough *right now*. If you want to lose weight or tone up, that's fine, but please don't wait until you're your 'perfect size' to be happy. That is such a waste of time.

I remember being on holiday in Spain many years ago and I thought I was big at the time (I wasn't). It rained for the entire week and I was glad because it meant that I didn't have to show my bottom by the pool or on the beach. Isn't that ludicrous? I was actually pleased the weather was terrible because it meant I could hide away. I look back on that now and I'm ashamed of myself.

I certainly feel better, healthier and have more energy now I'm the size and shape I'm supposed to be, but if I tried to shed more pounds I would be back in that horrible prison of yo-yo dieting. I refuse to go back there. I'm now more comfortable with my size and I've stopped trying to hide behind clothes that cover my arms and my bottom. It is a joy to walk into a shop and try on clothes because I love them and to finally be able to tuck a crisp white shirt into my jeans.

APPRECIATING MY BODY

I've thought differently about my body ever since the horse-riding accident I had when I was 52. It hugely affected my confidence, but it proved to be a turning point and forced me to take better care of myself.

The accident happened when I was learning to ride as part of a charity challenge in 2012. I'd never ridden a horse in my life because I'd always been nervous of how powerful they are, and the one I was on was a big beast. The instructor suggested I should try a jump. It wasn't exactly Grand National-sized, but the horse knew he had a nervous passenger on his back, so he stopped dead and I fell off. The horse then reared up and his hoof, with that heavy metal shoe, came crashing down on my right thigh.

It's odd, but in my head I thought that because I was doing something for charity nothing bad would possibly happen. That was my logic, but it obviously didn't work out like that. I knew right away I was in trouble because of the pain and amount of blood coming from my leg. I was rushed to A&E in an ambulance and the paramedics were worried I could have damaged my pelvis and back as well. The horse's hoof missed my artery by millimetres, so I was incredibly lucky, but I still had to have an emergency operation, during which I was given three pints of blood. There was a lot of muscle and nerve damage and it took about an hour and a half in total for them to stitch me back up.

I was looked after incredibly well in A&E and then on the

ward, and I am so thankful to the wonderful men and women who work in our NHS. The treatment I got was amazing; everyone at St George's Hospital in London looked after me so well. And no, it wasn't just because I happen to be on the telly, it's because the NHS staff are caring, decent people and we are so lucky to have them.

I was in shock, but do remember as I was being wheeled into the operating theatre, whispering worriedly to my friend and producer Emma Gormley, that I probably wouldn't be in work tomorrow. I was in St George's for a week and then spent over a month recovering at home.

Steve managed to get me back to our house in Scotland by hiring a big car and bundling me up in a duvet and pillows. I had to take six weeks off work in total, and I found that really tough. As someone who is used to being constantly busy, it was frustrating suddenly having all that time when I was not able to do anything at all.

Steve cooked me hearty, healthy meals to get my iron levels back up after all the blood I'd lost, and he and Rosie took such great care of me. I had to rely on him totally – I even had to have help to get to the toilet and to shower. I've always been independent so it was hard to come to terms with that. The whole experience gave me a small insight into what it must be like to live with a disability, and I have a special respect and admiration for the tenacity of disabled people and the kindness of their carers.

I was prescribed Tramadol in hospital for the pain, but a few weeks after I got home I had to stop taking it because it's just too seductive. It made me feel completely numb and as if my head was full of cotton wool. If Steve had burst into the room and told me that the house was on fire, I would have just smiled woozily. The pain was intense without the strong drugs, but I preferred that to feeling disconnected. I can see how people get hooked on prescription drugs; they make you feel as though nothing really matters. Instead, I took paracetamol and other over-the-counter painkillers to take the edge off the pain.

I'd heard that physical ailments can have a big knock-on effect on your mental health, but I didn't realise just how much until my accident. I had to admit to myself that I wasn't invincible, and my body is just as fragile as everyone else's. It just shows that our lives can change in a heartbeat.

I couldn't look at the wound because I didn't want to have to face how hideous it was, so every time the nurses changed my dressing I turned away. The first time I was brave enough to look at it I burst into tears. Despite all the incredible work the surgeon did I was left with a massive curved scar on my right thigh. It looks like I've been bitten by a shark and there are a lot of lumps and bumps, which is inevitable with such a serious injury.

For a long time I thought the scar was horrific, and when I looked at myself in the mirror it was the first thing I saw, although everyone assured me it was nowhere near as bad as I thought. I used to cover it up with a sarong if I was on holiday, and I wouldn't wear tight jeans or leggings because I was so self-conscious about the bumpy bulge.

The scar still aches a little bit if the weather is cold, and I describe it as like having a very deep toothache, but other than that it doesn't give me any bother. I appreciate what a lucky escape I had not to have been killed, paralysed or left with more permanent damage. People have to deal with a hell of a lot worse.

Once I started to recover, I was desperate to get back to normal so I had physiotherapy twice a week to try to keep my leg as flexible as possible. I also started exercising as part of my rehab. I'd fallen off the exercise wagon a bit before the accident, and I needed to get my leg working again as soon as possible, and that's when I knew I needed to find exercise that I enjoyed.

Anyone who works shifts knows that it plays havoc with your eating patterns, because you're out of sync with the rest of the world and you often have to eat on the go. I'm up so early that by 11am I'm 'hangry' and I want my lunch, and I have my dinner by 6pm at the latest.

My problem was snacking. I was constantly reaching for the treats that are left out for us in the Green Room at work; I'd be eating croissants smeared with peanut butter and all sorts. But after I had my accident I realised that in order to heal quickly, I had to put good things into my body and help it along. I also realised that because I was inevitably moving around a lot less when I was first recovering, if I went back to my old eating habits I would end up the size of a house. So my accident actually changed the way I look at my body and made me realise that I had to start taking better care of myself.

EXERCISE

Make a list of all the things your body does that you are
grateful for, and all the things you love about it.

My body is great because . . .

_____

_____

_____

_____

_____

_____

_____

_____

FINDING WHAT WORKED FOR ME

After my accident, I had to accept that if I wanted to get my confidence back, it was going to require effort. In the first few weeks after I got home from hospital I felt wiped out, and it would have been easy to give in and spend all day lying on the sofa. I was knackered, and I remember Doctor Hilary telling me that exercise makes you less tired. I thought he was being utterly ridiculous and I said to him, 'I don't have the energy to walk to a class, let alone take part in one.' He promised me it would work. Annoyingly, as always, he was absolutely right.

Finding a way of exercising that worked for me and that I actually enjoyed was essential. A year after my accident, I went on holiday to Spain to see Joyce, who was living over there, and she dragged me kicking and screaming to a Zumba class. I thought we were going to spend our time together eating tapas and guzzling Rioja, but she was evangelical about this class and she certainly looked in the best shape of her life. Although I had to take it a bit easier than everyone else, I had such a lot of fun.

As soon as I got home I looked for the nearest exercise class to me, and I found one in my local church hall five minutes' walk away. I was a bit nervous going for the first time because I was on my own and didn't know anyone. I was also worried I wouldn't be able to keep up, but I realised right away that everyone takes things at their own pace and they are far more concerned with themselves than looking at me.

As anyone who watches my show will know, the class instructor was the force of nature that is Maxine Jones, and her energy and enthusiasm made me feel happy and relaxed straight away. She changed my life, and I eagerly look forward to my classes with her. They are good for the body, the mind and the soul.

Sometimes I'll go to my class feeling really tired and stressed out, but after a few numbers I feel terrific. It's such a joy and a brilliant way of getting a natural high. You feel so much better about yourself after a right good workout. The camaraderie in class is terrific, too, and when you are having such a good time, who cares if you're a bit sweaty or you have some wobbly bits?

Once I started to feel better in myself and see my body change, it spurred me on and I didn't want to fill myself up with rubbish and junk food. In years gone by I could not eat chocolate without scoffing an entire family-sized bar, or have just the one biscuit from a packet, but now I can have what I want, walk away and leave the rest in the fridge or the tin, because I know that a little bit of what you fancy is fine, but too much will make you feel miserable.

I don't snack nearly as much as I used to, or eat mindlessly. There's nothing wrong with snacking as long as you're eating the right things, though, so I make sure I have some raisins and nuts to prevent me automatically grabbing a cake.

I used to think, 'Wouldn't it be lovely if there was something that was healthy and came in a handy package so I could eat it really quickly?' Then I realised that thing already exists, and it's called a banana, so I always have one of those to hand, too.

The amount I eat has also changed. Steve is a brilliant cook but he has no concept of portion control. He'll pile our plates high with food and I could eat the lot without giving it a second thought, so it's up to me to be sensible and not overeat. I also eat more slowly nowadays, which makes it much easier to know when I've had enough.

What has worked for me, long term, is combining eating well with doing exercise that I love. It's so basic it almost feels too easy. No more weighing food, furtively checking the back of packets for the calories and fat content or skipping meals. Why didn't someone tell me about this when I was 16?!

To be 60 and be in the best shape of my life feels incredible, and while I think exercise is something we all need to do, please don't take that to mean that you have to start training for a marathon tomorrow. Start small; go for a little walk, put on your favourite music and dance about in your living room, run up and down the stairs a few times. Do some squats in front of the TV. Try an online yoga tutorial. Do anything that will get you up off the sofa and help you to feel better. If you're lucky enough to come across an instructor like Maxine who makes every class a joy, then even better.

Exercising has obviously helped me to tone up, get the unhealthy weight off and keep it off, but even more importantly it's helped my head. You just feel better when you exercise. It's almost like giving your brain a clear-out and getting rid of all the toxic thoughts. It's a way of hoovering out your insecurities and anxieties.

Just going for a walk improves my mood. Most of us are within walking distance of a park, and getting out in the fresh air is so good for the soul. Start with a small stroll and go from there.

If I'm on my own I will often phone friends for a chat and a catch-up when I'm out and about with Angus, and the time flies by. I'll look down at my watch and I can't believe how long I've been going for. Walk with someone whose company you enjoy and you'll be surprised how quickly time passes. I guarantee you'll be on a high when you get back home.

EXERCISE

How should you exercise when you hate exercise? Use these questions to help figure out how to incorporate more exercise into your life.

- **What forms of exercise haven't you tried?** *Experiment. It might sound obvious, but if you don't try something, you don't know whether you'll like it or not. I had no idea exercise classes would turn out to be so life-changing until I gave them a shot. If you love music, Zumba or spin would be ideal for you, but if you prefer things to be more low-key, yoga, Pilates or swimming will be more up your street.*

- **Do you prefer to exercise indoors or outdoors?** *If you hate exercising indoors, but like classes, check to see whether any take place in your local park.*

- **Do you prefer to exercise in a group environment or on your own?** *Some people feel more motivated in classes, while others like sticking their headphones on and getting into the zone in the gym. Or work out with a friend, that way you can encourage each other when one of you can't be bothered (and you'll get to catch up with the gossip).*

- **When is it easiest for you to exercise?** *Be realistic. There's no point in promising yourself you'll go to a class at 8pm when you know full well you'll get in from work and flop down on the sofa. Choose classes or schedule in gym visits at a time when you know you'll actually do them and try to stick to a routine.*

- **Be patient. Don't give up when you don't get instant results. They will come!**

THE LIFE-CHANGING
MAGIC OF MAXERCISE

My life changed when I discovered Maxine's exercise classes back in 2013. Her energy and enthusiasm had me hooked from the word go, and I've found that working out helps to keep me sane. I hope this interview with her will inspire you to get active, too!

Why is exercise so important?

It's my answer to absolutely everything. I've always needed and wanted to exercise, and I walk out of a class feeling ten feet tall. One of the best things you can do for your physical, emotional and mental health is to get yourself moving.

How did you end up as a Zumba teacher?

In 2010, I was bullied out of my job in the city, I went through a really hard time. I was depressed and I hadn't been out of the house for weeks when a friend offered to take me to a Zumba class. I'd never experienced anything like it and it proved to be the thing I needed to get my life back on track. I loved it so much I became an instructor. I soon morphed away from Zumba and have created my own brand – MaxiciseTV with music from the club scene and of course the '80s, the decade I grew up in. The magic is in the music; it brings people together. I love helping women get the most out of exercise and discover the joy of dance aerobics, it's pure joy.

As you mentioned, the mental health benefits of exercise are fantastic.

Exercise does make you look better, but how it makes you feel is just as important. The feel-good hormones that are released when you exercise are incredible.

There's also a massive social element to any dance class that shouldn't be overlooked. Loneliness is at the centre of a lot of mental health problems, so just getting out and into a class can make all the difference. You might be a shy person, but saying hello to someone you recognise from the week before might really perk you up. It stops you from feeling so alone and when you meet like-minded people you feel that you are a part of something.

It's hard to get motivated if you've been out of the exercise loop for a while, but at the end of the day we've got to get off our backsides and make a start, haven't we?

Absolutely. We all want something, but we're not always prepared to go all-out to get it. Sometimes we can't be bothered, but that holds us back so much. I've written 'be bothered' on my bedroom mirror so that I see it every morning.

We live in a lazy society where we can get our food cooked for us or our shopping delivered, but no online store can deliver you toned arms or the post-exercise buzz. We can't expect everything to be instant, we need to put in some effort and be invested. You can't expect to go to the gym for a month before your holiday and be set for life. It doesn't work like that. But if you commit to exercise in the long term, you will get results.

Lorraine Kelly

Some people don't feel like they're worth making that effort for, do they?

Some people feel defeated before they even try. I think we can set ourselves unreasonable goals and read too many women's magazines where pictures are airbrushed and it's not real life. We're all different shapes and sizes and that's how it *should* be.

Some people have low self-esteem and think that because they'll never look like a model, there's no point in working out. But you watch their self-esteem rocket once they start toning up and become a part of something. I'm not here to make people skinny, I want to make them fit, happy and healthy. You need to change the narrative when you look in the mirror and say to yourself, 'I'm doing this for me, not because of what other people think about me.'

We have to accept that we're not going to look like a supermodel.

We need to be nice to ourselves. If you're constantly critical of your body you'll never be happy. I've got a little tummy on me and I always will have. I've done fad diets in the past and lost weight and my little tummy was still there. I looked bony and it didn't suit me and my tummy was still the same shape. I've learned to love my tummy now.

I've put my body through a lot of dancing and slam-dunking over the years, and if that's what it wants to look like, I'm going to respect it. It's served me well and I'm embracing it. Loving yourself is the most powerful thing you can do for yourself. Every morning, look at yourself in the mirror and say, 'Morning gorgeous, we're going to have a fabulous day today!' It lightens your mood. You need to be your own best friend. It all starts with self-love.

How long does it take for people to get back into exercising after a break?

It takes three weeks for the brain to accept a new habit, so try going to a class three times a week for three weeks. Schedule it in your diary – no excuses – and it will become a habit. Once you've done that, move on to the next thing. Maybe cut out having biscuits for your 10am snack or stop having sugar in your tea. Quit your bad habits one at a time, and do each thing for at least three weeks to give your brain a chance to adapt. Break it down and do one thing at a time so it's manageable. I get people to write down a list of their bad habits and then decide which one they want to work on first. It's about prioritising.

We've become very all or nothing . . .

We have. If you make rules you can't stick to you will go up and down in peaks and troughs. You'll fall off the wagon and you'll feel like a failure, then you'll probably give it up altogether. That's what happens to people in the new year; they stop drinking and smoking, they join a gym and they go on a diet. It never lasts because it's too much for your brain. *Do one thing at a time.*

I still treat myself. I love a glass of wine with my dinner but I don't have one on a Monday, Tuesday and Wednesday. I'm allowed one the rest of the time if I fancy it. They are the rules and my brain accepts that's the way it is. I'm not restricting myself and saying I can never have wine again, but I'm not having it every night.

We can start exercising at any age, can't we?

We can! Actually, as we get older we become more accepting of ourselves and often we work out to be fit and healthy *as well as* look good.

Some people think you need to join a fancy gym to get in shape.

They do, but that's not the case at all. Some people believe that if they're financially invested they might be more inclined to go, and that may well work for some, but a lot of the time the gym membership will lapse and you'll be left with a big hole in your pocket. A walk or a run in the park costs nothing, and classes are often a total bargain. At the end of the day, it's what suits you and is going to make you want to get off that sofa.

Experiment and find out what you like. Some people love cycling or swimming. Just do it! You need to find something fun that's going to tempt you back. The feeling you get after working out is amazing and it will spur you on for next time. If you're in a class, the other people will spur you on. There are so many different ways to exercise, and you can start off slowly and build it up.

We can also work out at home if we're a bit shy?

Totally, it can be a great way to get started. Exercise at home and join a class when you feel more confident. If you find it works for you, carry on! I do a live stream so people can work out at home, but they're dancing with 70 other people and getting a great workout to banging tunes without leaving the house (see www.maxicise.tv for more info).

People think they need all the latest gear to work out in.

You absolutely do not. I hate that thing of having 'all the gear and no idea'. I certainly don't spend a fortune on my workout clothes, I get them from Amazon or eBay. I like bright, bold, colourful clothes because I want people to see me coming, but a lot of people prefer black clothes, because they make them feel slim and safe, which is totally fine, too.

If you want to splash out on fancy gym gear because it will make you want to go more, do whatever it takes, but the only thing I spend a lot of money on is trainers. They're the most important item because wearing bad trainers can be harmful to your body. Also, a decent sports bra is essential too. Aside from those two things, you can wear an old T-shirt and leggings and your workout will be every bit as good. You're only going to end up a sweaty mess anyway, so wear what makes you feel comfortable.

We need to stop worrying about how we look when we're working out.

To look good, you need to sweat. I always say if you want to look good on the beach you need to look bad when you're exercising. You need to be sweaty and red. That's what goes into you looking and feeling fabulous. There is nothing sexier than a confident woman, but to get to that place you need to look a bit dodgy at times.

You're not one for bathroom scales, are you?

No. We're all different heights and shapes with varying bone densities. As long as I'm happy in my clothes I don't care what the scales say. I love eating; I like the social element and I think good food is amazing. Food is beautiful. So eat well and drink well but be nice to your body and don't fill it with rubbish. I'll cook fresh salmon and wholegrain rice. I eat fruit and a lot of vegetables and salads, and that's my lifestyle now. I'm sensible but I'm not depriving myself. I want to eat those things.

It took me a little while to get to that place but now I eat well because I want to feel good, not because I'm dieting. I have curry once a week and I love a drink and that's what real life is. I'm not pretending I'm perfect. I don't eat things like ready meals or white bread because they have no nutritional value. I generally avoid sugar, but I do have one in tea, but I only have one cup a day. I think sugar is more addictive than cocaine and it's very hard to give up. Apart from tasting nice, it's got no redeeming qualities. The energy that comes from sugar is bad calories. Our bodies burn fat better than they do sugar.

So you don't diet but you do watch what you eat?

Yes, because it's all about balance and you don't want to go one way or the other. If you feed yourself well it makes all the difference. You need to eat breakfast; a protein breakfast will sustain you all morning and stop you reaching for biscuits at 10.30am. Then have carbs with lunch – something like a jacket potato with protein, or protein and vegetables with wholegrain rice will see you through until dinner. Then for dinner, cut down your carbs and have vegetables and protein and your body will burn that off as you sleep.

Do a good diet and exercise have to go together?

For me, they do. I want to look after my body. We're living to a much older age now and I want to give my body the best chance of survival. When I retire I want to be able to go out and see the world, and that's why I'm taking care of myself every day.

Eat well and move your body and you will feel better. It's so simple. If you treat yourself well, you'll have a happier, healthier life. Life is so much nicer when you feel good.

EXERCISE

Write down a list of the habits you would like to tackle, then rank them in order of importance. Work on kicking one habit at a time, taking three weeks to do it, then start on the next one and so on. Don't try to tackle them all at once – one thing at a time is more likely to be sustainable.

_____

_____

_____

_____

_____

_____

_____

STYLE

Once you're happy with your body, I bet you'll soon be more confident with your style. My own style journey has been a bit of a learning curve, but thankfully I've had some great help along the way.

I'VE HAD MY FAIR SHARE OF STYLE MISHAPS

I must admit that now my body has settled, going into a shop and picking up something off a rail and knowing it will fit is a great feeling – especially when you can choose to wear something because you like it and not just because you think, 'Is this going to hide my bum or skim the bits of my body I don't like?'

I spent so many years using clothes to hide parts of my body that I hated. I'm not even sure whether clothes do look better on me now, but I feel better in them, and that's the difference. It's not about being a perfect size 10 or 12, it's about wearing clothes you love with flair and a smile, and enjoying them.

My style has changed so much over the years – and it really needed to! I liked to think I was a bit of a style maverick when I was younger. I vividly remember buying black tights and ripping holes in them during the punk rock phase. Then I was a born-again mod for a while and I stole my dad's parka jacket and sewed target patches on it that I'd ordered from the back of *NME*. When the New Romantic era came in I wore black trousers, a red cummerbund and a massive white shirt with billowing sleeves, like a member of Spandau Ballet. Then I went through a phase of dressing like Robert Smith from The Cure.

I went through a big transformation when I became the Scottish correspondent for *TV-am* because I had to look like a proper grown-up when I was in front of the camera. I was filming outside most of the time, so I generally chose clothes that would keep me warm and dry, and as I'd often get a call in the middle of the night asking me to go and cover a story, I'd just have to grab whatever was sensible and weatherproof.

My appearance was the last thing on my mind at these times, but I had to look acceptable without being flashy or distracting because the last thing in the world you want as a news reporter is for people to be looking at your lurid scarf or scruffy coat rather than listening to the story you are telling.

I didn't have anyone helping me with my wardrobe when I started on the *TV-am* sofa, and I made so many blunders. I was very much the girl next door of breakfast telly, so I thought it was fine to wear big jumpers and sensible frocks. My then boss, Bruce Gyngell, also had a thing about bright colours, so the entire presenting team looked like Dolly Mixtures. I had a jacket that I've kept that has one green sleeve, one yellow one and the body is multicoloured. It's like Joseph's coat of many colours and is truly dreadful (it's definitely not one of those things that might one day come back into fashion). I also wore enormous jackets with shoulder pads that made me look like Arnold Schwarzenegger, tight black pencil skirts and high heels I couldn't walk in. It was all about power dressing and the whole look was ageing.

My hair was so backcombed and hairsprayed then that it looked like a helmet that had been lowered onto my head every morning. I swear it wouldn't have moved if a hurricane had blasted through the studio. As for my make-up, well, it was the eighties, so I wore far too much blusher and heavy eye shadow that, again, put years on me. No wonder people say I look younger now than I did back then.

When I became pregnant, my outfits got even worse. No thought went into my clothes, I wore whatever fitted and covered me up. I did a lot of 'safe dressing' and wore what I felt comfy in. Nothing matched and I put on the same things over and over and over again. Once I found something I could fit into, it became a staple. After Rosie was born I was so short of time it was a case of grabbing what I could when I went shopping. I'd do fashion segments on screen while looking like I'd snatched the last thing left on a bargain rail.

Throughout my 40s I was Mrs Cardigan. You could not get me out of the damn things. I wore them on air, off air, around the house. They were my frumpy safety blanket. I looked like an unmade bed. Why did no one tell me? As I had a lifestyle where I wasn't going out much I only really had one posh frock that I would recycle time and time again, and as a result I didn't really discover what suited me until I hit my early 50s.

Rosie was the one who first helped me to find my style. She showed me that I didn't have to settle for an elasticated waistband. I didn't realise quite how frumpy I had become, and how much I was hiding myself away, until she encouraged me to experiment a bit more.

Nowadays I work with an amazing stylist called Bronagh, who helps me choose outfits and work out what suits me and what doesn't. I still find the whole red-carpet thing utterly terrifying. I'm always the one getting ready in the toilet with five minutes to spare, and I never feel as glamorous as everyone else. Even now I don't know how to stand still and pose. It's intimidating

when you've got all those cameras pointed at you, but I definitely feel more confident knowing I'm wearing something that fits me properly and hopefully won't land me on the 'worst-dressed' pages of magazines.

Sometimes other people are much better at seeing what suits you than you are. Bronagh is very good at knowing what works with my shape. She'll show me something on the hanger and I won't be sure, but she'll encourage me to try it on and I'm usually pleasantly surprised. Or I'll mention a dress I like and I can see from her face that she's not keen. I trust her judgement completely and she is always spot-on.

I used to play it so safe, and Bronagh has taught me not to be afraid of any shops no matter how young and trendy the other clientele. You can totally still go to River Island when you're 60 and beyond. Why not? I have become braver with age; I guess it's about knowing your limits. When those see-through trousers came into fashion I was never going to rush out and buy a pair, but I'll happily buy a T-shirt or skirt from Topshop.

When I was young, women in their 60s wore safe, shapeless clothes, unflattering comfortable shoes and wheeled a trolley around the shops, but it's so different now. We can wear what the heck we like, and quite right too.

I'm not a slave to fashion and I think it's wrong to follow a trend if it doesn't suit you. Obviously still experiment and have fun, but I think it's a mistake to bow to pressure and be a fashion victim. I mean, who decides that yellow is suddenly cool? And does that mean that you have to dress head to toe in yellow to look good? Not at all. As stylist Mark Heyes says, you can make a simple nod to a trend by getting a yellow handbag or shoes, but you don't have to spend your days looking like a ripe banana.

If it wasn't for my job, I would hardly have any of the clothes that I wear for work. All of my clothes are from the high street, and when I can no longer shut the wardrobe at work, I have a clear-out for 'Help for Heroes' and other charities.

I'm not big on jewellery. I've got one pair of earrings because I've got only got one pair of ears, and the only rings I wear are my engagement and wedding ones. I'm surprisingly low-maintenance and I would rather spend my money on holidays or things for the home than designer clothes and shoes. I've bought some daft things in the past that I think deep down I knew I would

never wear. I've splashed out on heels that killed me in the shop, but I somehow convinced myself I'd wear them in.

Most of the high heels I own have never touched concrete because they haven't ever left the studio. They're like house cats that never get to go outside. I live in flat shoes when I'm off air, because I am just not good at walking in heels. However, I do think that the right pair of heels can pull an outfit together and are so flattering. So I change from my flats into my heels just before we go on air, and then as soon as the show is over I'm back in my comfy shoes again. While I admire women who wear high heels every day, I don't know how they bear the fierce burning on the soles of their feet and the pain of crushed toes.

I treated myself to a pair of Christian Louboutin shoes for my 50th birthday and I wore them when I presented the Millies, which are *The Sun*'s military awards. People said to me afterwards, 'It was so lovely the way you held on to people's hands whenever they came up on stage.' Well, it was partly because I was putting them at ease, but it was also because of my high heels – I was wobbling around all over the place and they were effectively propping me up!

Lesson learned: don't sacrifice substance for style, and wear shoes that you can stand up in for more than five minutes.

On your next shopping trip, go out of your way to try clothes in colours, shapes and lengths that you'd never normally wear. Go into a shop you usually avoid. If it all feels too overwhelming, try online shopping or accessories. You can refresh stale outfits and make a statement with only a new bracelet or handbag.

MY STYLE ICONS

I think Meghan Markle has beautiful fashion sense, and Kate Middleton always gets it right, although her position means she has to play it a bit more safe. I love how Dame Helen Mirren will wear a designer dress and then throw a black leather jacket over the top of it to make it look really cool and modern. I wish I had some of my mum's style and class, and certainly my daughter's. Something may not have hanger appeal but Rosie can look at it and know it will look great on. I don't have that ability.

I like fashion to be comfortable and I don't like too much fuss. I keep things simple and stick to the basics. I like clean lines. I love a classic shirt dress. I feel very comfortable in those, both on air and off. And also wrap dresses – they're amazing on curvy women, and if you feel like you don't have much of a shape they give you one.

If you've got those staples, you can mix and match. I think we all need to start looking after our clothes and help them last longer. If you invest in some key pieces, you can easily add to that, but you'll need to buy less.

My fuss-free capsule wardrobe would include:

- *A jersey wrap dress*

- *A couple of shirt dresses*

- *A pair of chinos*

- *A light blue cotton shirt*

- *A classic white shirt and a pair of black cigarette trousers like Uma Thurman wears in* Pulp Fiction

- *Smart flat shoes*

- *A pair of back high heels*

- *A pair of nude high heels*

What's your signature style?

	Seek out	Neutral	Avoid
Colours			
Shapes and styles			
Shops			

MAKE YOUR STYLE SHINE

Bronagh Webster is my brilliant stylist. I've learned so much from her since we started working together; she has pushed me out of my style comfort zone – and she finally got me out of those frumpy cardigans!

First things first, Bronagh, how can we work out what actually suits us best?

There are no hard-and-fast rules, it all depends on what you feel comfortable in. Just because something is in fashion doesn't mean it's going to suit your shape, size or personality. Feeling good in what you wear is the most important thing – *that* is what suits you. Always accentuate your favourite assets, whether that is your bum, waist, collarbone, wrists or anything else! Let the part of your body that you love the most be the focal point of your dressing.

You can tell whether someone is comfortable in what they are wearing, because clothes can have a massive effect on how you feel and how you appear. The number one rule is to make sure you feel comfortable before you leave the house. The chances are, if you don't feel good in front of the mirror at home you are not going to magically feel better at a wedding two hours later. Don't ever think 'it will be fine'; for big events, try on your outfit, including your shoes, shapewear, hats and accessories, at least a week before you plan to wear it, that way you have plenty of time to tweak what you are not happy with. Whatever you do, don't leave this to the last minute; a change made in a panic can be disastrous. If you have an emergency, revert to an old favourite rather than picking a risky option.

Are we all making ourselves look worse by trying to cover up in baggy clothes?

Absolutely. Sadly, by trying to cover up the bits of your body you're not comfortable with, by wearing smocks, tent-like tops or very baggy jeans, you're almost highlighting them. We need to embrace what we've been given and make the most of it. As cheesy as it may sound, it's about self-love and self-confidence. All of us have safety-blanket clothes for the days when we don't feel so good, and that's fine, as long as we don't get into a routine of wearing them every day.

Are there any clothes that are particularly flattering and slimming?

Steer attention away from the area you are most self-conscious about by wearing print pattern elsewhere. So if you're not keen on your top half, wear print on the bottom, and vice versa. You basically want to highlight the parts that you're most confident about. Ruching on dresses flatters tummies, and wide-leg trousers are very slimming and flattering. You can't go wrong with a good suit either, because you can dress it up or down. It's a chic option for events and suits look very cool when dressed down with a basic T-shirt and trainer. Plus you can then wear the jacket and trousers separately, so a well-cut suit is a brilliant investment.

We're all a bit scared of bright colours and we tend to go for a safe option, which is usually black.

There's nothing to be frightened of! Colour is amazing; if you're feeling a bit glum it can instantly lift your face and overall look. Find a colour that suits your skin tone and it can really complement your features.

As I know all too well, it's very easy to get stuck in a style rut . . .

There's nothing wrong with having your go-tos. We tend to experiment more when we are younger and it can be hard to break free from a 'style rut'. It's common to become complacent and avoid taking risks. I would always advise spending time and money on a strong capsule wardrobe. A store of reliable, quality basics makes it easier to introduce new trends. It costs nothing to try something new in a shop, and an item that might initially feel intimidating could potentially become a new staple for you. If in doubt, give it a go. You have nothing to lose.

How closely should we follow the latest trends?

It's about experimenting while knowing your limitations. Don't wear something *just* because it's on-trend; not all trends suit everyone and there's nothing wrong with that. As I said, if you have a strong capsule wardrobe you can add current trends to suit your own style. There are so many different trends each season, you don't have to wear them all. And certainly not all at the same time . . .

I dress people in outfits that they never would have tried on, and they can be stunned at how good they feel in them. You might find that one new thing that will totally suit your body shape and revitalise your wardrobe. For instance, so many people think they can't wear a jumpsuit, but actually they can look great on many shapes and sizes. There are so many different styles, there really is something for everyone. Jumpsuits are such an easy piece to wear because they're a complete outfit. For me, they stand next to the 'little black dress' as a classic, easy win.

You should spend more on your capsule wardrobe and less on fast-fashion items. The on-trend pieces may not be in style for long so the likelihood is that you're not going to get much use out of them, whereas a good pair of jeans can last forever. I'd say the key items to have in your wardrobe are a decent pair of jeans, an everyday blazer and some good-quality camis and T-shirts. It sounds silly suggesting that people invest in something as simple as a T-shirt, but they are wardrobe game-changers. They're vital, and if you spend a little bit more on these basics that fit well and keep their shape, you'll have them for years. It's all about finding the ones that suit your body shape. Never underestimate your wardrobe basics.

What's the secret to finding a great pair of jeans?

There isn't a secret, I'm afraid, it's all about trial and error. I wish there was a secret formula; however, it totally depends on your shape, size and leg length. Some stores have petite and tall ranges and there are some fabulous plus-size brands out there, too. As we all know, one size never fits all, but if you discover a certain brand of jeans that fit you well, the chances are their other jeans will too because they'll be a similar cut. If you find a pair that you really, *really* love, double up and get a second pair. Jeans are always going to be in fashion and they are our most lived-in item for many of us.

And you know I love a wrap dress . . .

Wrap dresses are so flattering for pretty much all shapes and sizes. They cinch you in at the waist and highlight the right bits. They work for any occasion, they can be dressed up or down, and they are so easy to bung in a suitcase when you go away. A printed dress distracts the eye and takes attention away from any lumps or bumps. Vertical stripes work particularly well, and a small ditzy print is better than a large one because it's more subtle and won't draw attention to certain areas.

Is shapewear essential?

Absolutely, I always recommend it, regardless of size, because it creates a fabulous smooth silhouette. Again, I would recommend you invest in good shapewear – it's not something that you would wear every day so it can last forever. I would always go for a seam-free, no-VPL set as the knicker line won't dig in and it will create a smooth, flush line.

Shapewear is notorious for rolling up, so my top tip is to spray the bottom of it with hairspray to prevent it budging. Hairspray is also great for tackling static material if a top or dress is clinging to you. A light spray underneath the fabric will soon sort that out.

Do you recommend splashing out on a designer pair of shoes or a bag?

If you can, why not? Investment pieces can be worn well with pretty much any high-street look, and can make all the difference. There are so many amazing designer-inspired pieces available, there is no need to splash out on anything hugely expensive. You can look fantastic in a £30 dress, but it is nice to mix and match things with a designer shoe or handbag. If you are going to invest in clothes, go for something classic like a Burberry trench coat that will never date, rather than something that will go out of fashion by next season. It can be hard to make the right decision, so I'd advise sticking to a classic colour palette of black, navy, nude, metallics and, perhaps surprisingly, red and leopard print. They work with most colours and styles.

I'm not one for over-accessorising, but if you're wearing a plain dress it's nice to add a statement earring or necklace. Sometimes less is more. If you're going to invest in jewellery, go for something classic.

Have you got any good tips for making high heels more comfortable?

For new shoes, I always score the soles with a cheese grater (as random as that may sound) because it stops them sliding on the first outing. Another top tip would be to rub a bar of soap on the inside of the heel. It creates a wax barrier that stops the shoes rubbing and prevents blistering, and it works on any kind of shoe. Most high-street chemists sell special cushions to pad the balls of your feet or heels, and these really do relieve the pain of heels!

How often should we clear out our wardrobes?

I organise my wardrobe each season and put the clothes I don't need into storage. I'll use that as an opportunity to cull the things that I haven't worn. If I haven't worn something all season, why am I holding on to it? Don't be too precious with your clothes if you find that you have lost your love for them. You'll only end up hoarding things for years, so let go and make room for new things.

MAKE-UP DOES NOT HAVE TO COST A FORTUNE

My amazing make-up artist Helen does my face and hair every day before I go on air, which is such a wonderful perk. I call her my miracle worker. She has all these magic products that really enhance your face. I didn't even know what a primer was until a few years ago, and I still wouldn't know if she hadn't literally filled me in.

One thing that I did recently that was a game-changer was clear out my make-up bag. I'd had it for years and when I went to visit Rosie in Singapore she was so horrified at the state of it she took me to Sephora and made me get some new stuff. I didn't buy any expensive brands, because you do not have to spend a fortune for quality – we all know you're really paying for the fancy packaging, and marketing campaigns. Instead, I bought things I liked and that worked well on me, and it was all really affordable. Now every time I open my make-up bag it makes me happy as it's all shiny and gorgeous. As I don't wear much make-up when I'm not on screen my products last for ages.

Off screen, I tend to follow the same routine I have for years. I wear a tinted moisturiser as a base and I always choose one that has sunscreen, which is so important even here in the UK and even in winter. I'll wear some light concealer under my eyes, and I love brown shades on my eyelids. I also use brown mascara and eyeliner these days because it's much softer than black.

I don't tend to wear strong lipsticks because I think they can be ageing, but I love a tinted lip balm.

I always have the following in my make-up bag:

- *Simple Kind to Skin Replenishing Rich Moisturiser*

- *No7 Protect & Perfect Intense Advanced Eye Cream*

- *Avon Anew Ultimate Multi-Performance Day Cream*

- *Dove Silky Nourishment Body Cream*

- *Bobbi Brown Skin Long-Wear Weightless Foundation in Beige 3*

- *Benefit Hoola Original Bronzer*

- *Clarins Joli Rouge Lipstick in Delicious Pink*

- *Vaseline Lip Therapy in Rosy Lips*

- *Maybelline Lash Sensational in Brown*

- *Urban Decay NAKED2 Eyeshadow Palette*

- *Yves Saint Laurent Touche Éclat Illuminating Pen*

eau de parfum

FRINGE BENEFITS

I committed one of my worst hair errors when I was 15. I went into a posh Glaswegian salon and asked for a full fringe because they were just coming back into fashion, and the stylist didn't understand at all. She gave me a really short, choppy, uneven fringe and then shaved a V into the back of my head. It was a very swanky and intimidating salon so I thought she must know what she was doing, but I was horrified. I was too scared to say anything and I even thanked her at the end – and gave her a tip!

The haircut was so expensive I couldn't afford to get the bus home so I walked all the way, crying. I went straight up to my bedroom and sobbed for hours. My mum came in and said, 'It's not that bad.' Then she went downstairs and said to my dad, 'Oh my god, you should see Lorraine's hair.'

I wore a headscarf to school the following day and I didn't take it off for a month. My hair grows quite quickly but that horrendous fringe took forever to grow out. It was *almost* as bad as the home perm I had when I was 12 that left me looking like Shirley Temple.

My hair was jet black when I was young but it's become lighter and lighter – with a bit of assistance. Your skin and hair colour can change as you get older so you need to adapt, and lowlights and highlights can make such a difference. They're also great for covering up grey hairs, so if you do decide to go grey, ash blonde or silver will make the change less of a shock. A few years ago, my mother decided to go grey and it really suits her. It's

very elegant and not at all ageing. It's a personal choice. I would always recommend a fringe of some kind. Not only does it frame the face, it also protects you from the sun and therefore from wrinkles!

You can't underestimate the power of a good haircut. I've seen people take years off just by changing their hairstyle. When we do makeovers on the show, we have the whole package – with fresh make-up and new clothes – but it's the haircut that makes women look younger and have more confidence.

Don't be afraid to talk to your hairdresser about what you want and get their advice about what suits you. And please don't think that just because you're of a certain age you can't have long hair. A lot of older women look amazing with long hair.

A good hair day may not solve all your problems but it helps!

MOISTURISE, MOISTURISE, MOISTURISE!

One thing my mum drummed into me when I was growing up was the importance of having a good skincare routine, advice that I'm so grateful for. She always said to me, 'Moisturise, moisturise, moisturise, and then moisturise some more,' and I really took that on board.

I'm very lucky that we have good skin in my family, so I've

never struggled with acne, but it can get very dry so I take good care of it.

Again, I don't spend a fortune on expensive brands. If you can afford it, fine, but I like to use supermarket brands or products from Boots that are unperfumed and as natural as possible.

Rosie sends me face masks from Singapore, and they're wonderful for putting the moisture back into your skin. The ones for under your eyes are amazing.

Don't forget to moisturise your neck and chest, too. You don't need to buy special creams for certain areas, I just use whatever I'm putting on my face. I do sometimes forget about moisturising my body, so I'm trying to get better at that. I'm very guilty of buying body moisturiser or cellulite cream and thinking it's going to work by osmosis. Apparently you have to actually take it out of the tub and rub it into your skin for it to actually work!

HOW TO GLOW . . .
WITH A LITTLE HELP FROM
THE BEAUTY COUNTER

Make-up maestro Helen Hand has been working with me for over 17 years. She has a never-ending wealth of beauty knowledge and is an expert at hiding dark under-eye shadows if I have an early morning start. Take it away, Helen!

SKINCARE

Achieving the perfect base is the most important part of a make-up routine. Before you even go near foundation, make sure your skin is even and clean and prepped. You wouldn't put food on a dirty plate!

Use a light cleanser in the morning. I follow this with ice-cold water to wake up and get the blood moving without over-stimulating my face. For night-time cleansing, I use a gentle creamy facial cleanser starting from the décolletage (upper chest area. Don't neglect this area as it's exposed as much as the face is) in small circular movements. Remove with a soft flannel or cotton wool, then tone and moisturise with night cream.

Always use a separate cleanser for your eyes and an oil-based product for waterproof make-up. Gently massage into the lashes to remove all the make-up without too much rubbing. Be gentle around the eyes and try to avoid heavy products. Skin in this area is about 40% finer than the rest of the face. Eye cream is essential because the ageing process starts when you are as young as 16! Eye cream or balm should last you a long time as you only need to use a rice-grain-sized amount each day.

Taking care of your skin is essential but it can be a trying task. The type of skin you have is largely hereditary, but it can also be impacted by lifestyle and environment, and some products can help to reverse signs of ageing or skin damage.

When preparing your skin, make sure your skincare routine and skincare products are suitable for your skin type. Some people use products just because their friends are using them, but they might not be doing anything for them so they won't get that radiant glow. While it may make all kinds of promises, the 'cream of the moment' may not work for you. If you want to try products before buying them, take small empty travel pots into a store and ask for samples so you can test them at home.

Choosing the wrong product can lead to skin reactions and can do more harm than good. If you're finding it difficult to work out what skin type you have, go and see a professional for a consultation and get recommendations for what would suit you.

When choosing products for dry, dehydrated, sensitive or anti-ageing skincare, look for a high percentage of key quality ingredients which are going to calm, hydrate, nourish and feed the skin. As a general rule, more expensive products will be higher in the concentrated active ingredients so they will work more intensely, meaning you will see quicker results. However, that isn't always the case, so do check labels carefully and try to test products before splashing out on anything expensive.

Whatever moisturiser you use, make sure it has an SPF. I use an SPF moisturiser every single day, no matter what time of year it is.

Here's my A–Z of skincare ingredients that can really make a difference:

- ***Almond and plant-based oils.*** *These are soothing and prevent dehydration. Almond oil is packed with Vitamin E.*

- ***Alpha hydroxy acids (AHA)*** *can reverse ageing effects and improve the skin surface by exfoliating. Shedding dead skin cells on a daily basis removes dull, lifeless-looking skin.*

- ***Antioxidants*** *work to prevent your skin cells from damage caused by the environment, and help to prevent wrinkles and age spots.*

- ***Beeswax*** *is anti-inflammatory, and its anti-bacterial properties are essential for fighting chapped skin during the winter and hot summer months. It also forms a protective wall by sealing in moisture without clogging pores.*

- ***Cocoa butter*** *hydrates and nourishes, improves elasticity and helps to heal scar tissue, marks and deep wrinkles. It also forms a protective barrier over the skin to hold moisture in.*

- ***Hyaluronic acid*** *is a nutrient that improves the appearance of skin texture and helps with tissue repair. It keeps skin hydrated and balanced without adding oil.*

- ***Magnesium*** *helps to reduce acne, and is also effective for joint and muscle pain.*

- ***Non-comedogenic*** *products have been specially tested to avoid clogging pores.*

- **Retinol** is a derivative of vitamin A and helps to reduce the appearance of lines, wrinkles, sun damage, dullness and sagging skin. It enhances collagen and elastin production, and repairs skin at its deepest level.

- **Shea butter** moisturises, tones and softens. It's anti-inflammatory and has healing properties, helping to calm irritated skin. It contains vitamins A, E and F, which restore elasticity and act as a natural SPF.

- **Silicate** penetrates deep inside the pores and removes excess oil and bacteria that build up.

- **Sulphur** is a natural effective oil absorber. It's also anti-bacterial, which helps prevent clogging.

- **Vitamin C** is a brilliant anti-ageing ingredient. It's packed with powerful antioxidants that enhance the skin's protection against the environment. It also boasts collagen protection to preserve skin tone and tightness.

- **Vitamin E** is healing and can be used for a variety of skin conditions, including acne, psoriasis and scarring. It's anti-inflammatory, which supports cell function. It's also a powerful antioxidant, making it effective at combating and reducing the effect of UV damage.

TREATMENTS

Treatments that offer results beyond the capabilities of skincare are becoming more and more popular. I'm not a fan of Botox or fillers because I find them much more ageing. Once you start down that road it can become addictive, which I've seen happen so many times. Look after your skin well and it will pay off more in the long run.

There are many different facials that help slow down the ageing process. These treatments should be done on a regular basis, just like going to the gym. Maintenance is key. I exfoliate and do a mini-facial at home every week, and once a month I have a professional facial, which I've done since I was 16, when I started training to be a beauty therapist and aesthetician.

Here are my current favourite non-invasive treatments :

- *Collagen wave is one of the most sought-after non-surgical facial treatments at the moment. Treatments speed up the collagen production at its deepest level during the facial in order to plump, contour and tighten the skin using radio frequency and ultrasound waves.*

- *Caci (Computer Aided Cosmetology Instrument) is another non-surgical facelift and has been used for over 20 years. It regenerates skin tissues and helps to repair collagen, which boosts the appearance of skin texture. It tones by using a micro-current machine that transmits electrical signals through the skin at a deeper level than you get with a hands-on, product-based facial. You can also buy a home-care Caci machine to maintain youthful-looking skin.*

- Like Caci, the **Nu Skin age LOC Galvanic Spa** *can be used at home. It uses self-adjusting currents and conductors to reduce dullness, and minimise fine lines and wrinkles. It also improves elasticity, detoxifies skin and boosts blood circulation and oxygen levels in the skin and body.*

- **The Cryo Facial** *is one of my favourite treatments. The treatment includes a lactobotanical peel, which uses Alpha-Hydroxy Acid (AHA) to exfoliate, hydrate and smooth the skin, and address pigmentation issues. The peel is followed by cryotherapy, which uses pressurised carbon dioxide at temperatures as low as -78°C. The result: firmer, tighter skin.*

FINDING THE PERFECT FOUNDATION

Skin is the first thing people notice so it's vital to get a good base for your make-up.

Always check make-up in natural light when you're shopping for foundation. Use the tester to put a bit on your jawline and smooth it down into your neck. Then go outside and check the colour in a mirror. I know you might look a bit weird, but it's worth it. I recommend the same for lipstick.

The magic of foundation is all in the blending. Don't forget about your neck. Generally, your neck doesn't get as much sun as your face and may be a bit lighter, so you need to blend foundation all the way down. We don't want to end up with that '80s look where faces and necks were totally different colours. We know better than that now!

Make-up shouldn't finish at your jawline.

Apply foundation using a brush or your hands. I prefer using a brush to a sponge because the latter absorb so much product you end up wasting half of it. For a light and dewy look, I use my fingertips, but avoid this if your hands are hot because your foundation will melt!

Avoid power if you have dry skin or want a bit of a glow. If you're oily, apply powder with either a brush or puff to set and hold foundation so it stays all day.

To hide blemishes, use a small, precise brush to apply concealer after putting on your foundation. Work it in with a light patting motion and repeat with your powder on the area to set make-up so it doesn't lift.

SHAPE, BRIGHTEN, COLOUR

Once you've achieved the perfect base, you can move on to the fun bit! Always make the most of your strongest features. Whether you have amazing eyes, full lips or fabulous high cheekbones, make them stand out. If you want to bring out your eyes, dab a little concealer right in the corner. For lips, you want to focus on your cupid's bow.

Highlighter does exactly what it says: it highlights areas. People sometimes put illuminators or highlighters too high up on the cheekbone into the eye area, where you can have laughter lines. Highlighter will exaggerate these and make them more obvious.

If you have a strong high-arched eyebrow and you want to make it stand out even more, you could add a little highlighter just under the brow. Or if you want to give the illusion you have a strong eyebrow, highlight the same area, which will have the same effect.

The secret to blusher and contouring is gradual build-up and blending. Contouring was very subtle when I was training but now it's very heavy. That might look good on Instagram tutorials when people have a big light shining on them, and it's fine if you look like Kim Kardashian, but it doesn't suit everyone. Some people get the colours wrong and it looks like they've got bruises down the sides of their faces.

Women say to me all the time that they can't wear eyeshadow colours like pink and blue, but there are so many shades and tones in every colour so don't limit yourself. Experiment! You will always find one that will suit you. Ask for advice from make-up experts on beauty counters, and if you're not sure about colours take empty pots with you and ask for samples. If you're going to be spending a lot of money on make-up, try it out at home first and make sure it works for you.

ANTI-AGEING

As we get older, we often need to adapt our routines to cater to changing face shape, texture and tone. It's easy to stick to old favourites, but ask yourself if you're using those products because they make you look great, or because it's easy?

If you don't have any blemishes, scars or pigmentation, keep the base, foundation and blusher light. No one looks good with cakey make-up, and it does bring out those lines, pores and puff that are common as we age. Add a little highlighter in the right places and your skin will look youthful, radiant, fresh and glowing.

Black mascara and eyeliner can look slightly hard on the face. You can soften make-up by either mixing the colour or using a lighter or brighter tone, like brown-black, black-purple or black-blue. Make sure your mascara doesn't look dry or clumpy because that is not a flattering look; negative attention to the eye area will also draw attention to eye bags or lines.

As we grow older, we can lose the pigment and volume in our eyelashes and eyebrows, which can really age us and make eyes seem faded. There are lots of amazing treatments that can help:

- **HD Brows**, *also known as High Definition Brows, uses a combination of tinting, waxing, threading and plucking to reshape and colour eyebrows.*

- **LVL** *treatment, which stands for length-volume-lift, lifts the lash straight up from the root without a kink or bend, giving the illusion of longer lashes. The treatment is completed with an eyelash tint to enhance and darken the colour of your eyelashes, so you don't need to use mascara.*

- *A more dramatic and invasive treatment is **semi-permanent make-up** or **microblading**, which is safe and can look fantastic. Ensure you have a patch test at least 24–48 hours beforehand. A thorough consultation by a reputable, highly-trained therapist is essential. For semi-permanent make-up, a cosmetic digital tattooing machine is used with a lower frequency to that of a regular tattoo machine. The pigment is implanted to the deeper layer of the skin to create or change the shape of your eyebrows.*

THE CAT EYE

The eyeliner flick is a timeless look that suits everyone and never goes out of style so it's worth spending some time mastering it.

- *The key is to get a fine-tipped liquid pen and follow the angle of your outer lashes outwards.*

- *Do the flick first and then draw a fine line along your upper lash. If you mess up you can use a cotton bud to even it out.*

- *If you're nervous about eyeliner pens, use a dark eyeshadow and a thin brush to create the illusion of an eyeliner, and then blend it into the rest of your eyeshadow.*

- *Experiment with thin and thick lines, and with different eyeliner brushes, to find what works best for you.*

SMOKY EYES

It might seem intimidating, but smoky eyes are probably the easiest make-up look! The classic technique is to use blacks and greys, but now you can use any colours.

My favourite smoky eye was created by my favourite make-up artist, the late Kevyn Aucoin:

- *Use a deep purple/plum colour all over the socket and just above*

- *To create the depth of colour, add a warm bronze all over the top and blend.*

- *To finish the look, add a black eyeshadow along the upper and lower lash line, like eyeliner (this doesn't have to be in a perfect line)*

- *Add two coats of mascara and you're done!*

Charcoal grey and black eyeshadow also work well with a black eyeliner for a simple look.

LASTING LIPPIE

Lipstick can turn a plain look into a glamorous one, but flaky lips and smudging can make people avoid it altogether. Here are the three simple steps to perfect lips:

- *Firstly, put a bit of moisturiser on your lips and then wipe them with a rough flannel to get rid of any dead skin.*

- *Next, line your lips with a lip liner and then fill in the rest of your lips with the pencil.*

- *Apply your lipstick over the top, seal it with a bit of translucent powder and it should stay put for hours.*

FAKING IT

Fake tan is an important part of lots of people's beauty routines, and with so many products available, it's possible to get a professional look in your own home. Just follow these steps:

- *Exfoliate your whole body and then shower to get rid of dry, dead skin. Make sure the water isn't too hot and give your skin a chance to cool down before you apply any product. If your skin is too warm or you perspire a lot when applying your tan, it can slide and create stripes.*

- *Wait a couple of hours after shaving before applying fake tan. Wait 24 hours after waxing as skin will be particularly sensitive and could react badly.*

- *Moisturise any areas that may be dry, or anywhere that bends, like your knees, your elbows and under your arms, so the product doesn't clump.*

- *Wear latex gloves with mitts over the top on both hands to apply tan evenly.*

- *Once you've applied the tan, wipe the soles of your feet and around your nails and wash your hands thoroughly.*

- *Don't forget to wash your eyebrows and under your nose. Even though they might be tiny areas, we've got little tiny follicles and the product can seep in. Use a wet flannel and gently brush in the opposite direction to the hairs to make sure those areas stay clump-free.*

- *To tan hands, take your gloves and mitts off and apply plenty of hand cream. Add a little tanning product to a mitt and rub it all over both hands and fingers. Wipe both palms and around the nail area thoroughly. Add a little more hand cream to avoid colour clogging around the fingers and knuckles.*

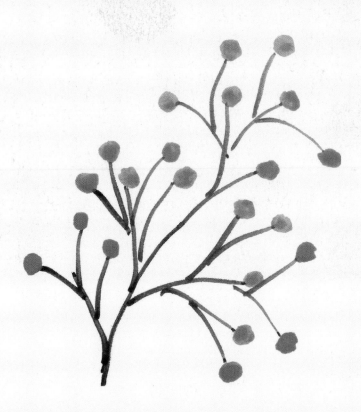

So there you have it – all my secrets on how to glow. Looking good is about putting yourself first. Don't ever feel guilty about that. Make-up, hair and clothes are often dismissed as frivolous or superficial, but, alongside a healthy lifestyle, a basic self-care routine will help you to both look good *and* feel confident.

DAZZLE

It's time to dazzle! In Spark and Glow, we looked at how you can nurture your mind and body. None of us exist in isolation though, so in this section, we'll look at how you can take your newfound confidence out into the wider world.

Like most people, my family and friends are everything to me, but when life moves fast, it can be easy to lose sight of that. Too often, we find ourselves distracted by the stresses of the day. While we each have our own responsibilities, it's also important to step back and take stock of the big picture, instead of firefighting problems as and when they come up, all day every day. Over the years, I've learned how important it is to stop for a little while and appreciate the golden moments.

That's not to say that work isn't an important part of my life. I'm lucky enough to have a job that I adore and that has provided many, many of my golden moments over the years. But I do think that's an exception rather than the rule.

Ultimately, in order to live your best life, you have to find your purpose and that might be your job, it might be building a comfortable home for you and your family or it might be travelling the world! All of these life purposes are equally valid; you just have to be honest with yourself and strict about prioritising your time and energy.

So, in this section, we'll be looking at how to improve your relationships, make a happy home, achieve your goals at work, and I hope to empower you to start making your dreams come true.

FRIENDSHIP

You can't shine without a little help from your friends. If you're feeling low, they are your first port of call. That might sound obvious, but there's a difference between an acquaintance, a mate and a true friend. They all have their part to play, but when it comes down to it, true friends are the secret to a happy life.

GOOD FRIENDS ARE PRICELESS

For me, a friend is someone you can phone at 3am about anything and they'll be there for you. It's someone who's got your back and will always fight your corner. It's someone you can trust with all of your secrets.

You need to know that if you told someone you'd done a terrible thing they would still be your friend. Instead of judging you they would say, 'Ok, how are we going to help you through this?' It's you and them against the world.

Friendship is give and take. You are each other's advisors. Sometimes you need to make sacrifices to be there for a friend, but it's never really a burden because you know they'd be there for you. None of us are happy all the time and if we're going through a tough patch we should be able to be honest about it and open up. That often brings you even closer together. You can share the good and the bad, and that forges an unbreakable bond.

The best friends are those who take you as you are. There are friends you know you need to hoover for if they are coming round, then there are those who won't judge you if your house is a bit untidy. It's so relaxing when you have that person in your life who you know won't mind if you only have cheap snacks and plain biscuits left in the tin to offer.

My best pal Joyce and I have been friends since we were 12 and we tell each other everything. We tell each other things we don't even tell our husbands. She lives abroad now, but we keep in touch all the time and even if we haven't seen each other for weeks, we just pick up the conversation as though one of us popped to the shops five minutes ago.

We all have different faces and different versions of ourselves for different situations. Whatever it is, no one is one hundred per cent themselves all the time. So when you find that person you can relax and feel completely comfortable with, you've struck gold. I remember Esther Rantzen saying to me that since her husband died she has had plenty of people to do lots of things with, but she has no one to do *nothing* with. I know exactly what she means. If you feel the same, know that you're not alone. Joyce and I may have met when we were kids, but golden friendships can come along later in life, too. Maxine and my pals in her class are perfect examples of that.

It's easier than ever to reconnect with old friends through social media; if you regret losing touch with someone who once made you feel good about yourself, be brave and drop them a line. Sometimes there's a reason why you're no longer friends, but rediscovering a connection can be very special.

Ultimately, what you need in a friend is someone who makes you laugh, someone you can guffaw with until it hurts, and that kind of closeness comes from shared experience. There's nothing quite like a friend from school or work that you've known for years. You can reflect on daft memories and relive them dozens of times and still find them funny, but equally you can have a giggle with someone you haven't known for long but who 'gets' you.

A proper belly laugh is so good for the soul. It relaxes you, releases endorphins (your body's feel-good hormones), boosts your immune system and (believe it or not) burns calories! If I could give people one piece of advice to make their lives better today, it would be to smile and laugh more, and to do that you have to be around people who make you happy.

EXERCISE

Think about the people you spend time with and divide the pie chart below accordingly. Who would you like to spend more time with? Make a new pie chart to reflect your goal and prioritise accordingly.

NO ONE IS IMMUNE
FROM LONELINESS

Loneliness is, sadly, increasingly common. The statistics are shocking. A study by the Co-op and the British Red Cross found that 9 million people across the UK are either always, or often, lonely. According to Age UK, 3.6 million older people live alone. Incredibly, loneliness can be as harmful to our health as smoking 15 cigarettes a day. Thankfully, more and more is being done to tackle this issue. The UK now has its first ever Minister for Loneliness.

I first experienced loneliness myself when we moved from Glasgow to East Kilbride when I was 12. I'd already spent a year at John Street Secondary in Bridgeton, so when I joined my new school everyone had already made their friends and I didn't know a soul. I was utterly miserable for about three months. I was totally on my own and felt like I was never going to make any pals. I thought no one would ever want to be my friend and that really affected my confidence. But then one day I started a conversation with a group of girls, including Joyce, and from that initial connection, a friendship grew.

I experienced loneliness again when I moved down to London when I was in my twenties. I didn't know a single person and it's such a vast city that I felt lost. The move was a huge culture shock for me. In Glasgow, everyone speaks to one another; if you stand at a bus stop, it's totally normal to strike up a conversation with someone you don't know to pass the time of day. Glaswegians are naturally inquisitive (some might even say cheekily nosy) and they don't think twice about asking you all sorts of questions about your life.

So I was used to walking down the street and saying hello to people whether I knew them or not, and suddenly I was in a place where no one looked at each other or acknowledged the existence of anyone around them, and where everything and everyone moves so fast. When I started chatting to people on the Tube or at bus stops in London they would mostly bristle and ignore me. I used to try to talk to people on the Underground and they clearly thought I was a bit deranged. I was just trying to be friendly.

I was so lonely I used to walk around London for hours on my own just for something to do. I also liked the fact that it tired me out so I could sleep, rather than lying in bed wondering if I'd made a terrible mistake moving away from everyone I knew and loved.

Whether it's moving to a new city, starting further education or getting a new job, leaving your support system behind can be scary. Loneliness gnaws away at you and you've got to make an effort to make friends, even though it's really difficult at first. Whenever I've moved anywhere I always go round to the neighbours and introduce myself, then I look for something to sign up to – whether it's a walking club or, for me, an exercise class. Going along to that first class can be a bit daunting when you don't know anyone, but the sense of camaraderie that builds up means you soon feel right at home, and it's a real boost to see the smiling faces of new friends you have made.

We all know you can be lonely in a crowded room. You can have lots of friends and a strong family, or be married and have kids, and you can still have those days where you feel like you're completely on your own. That's a normal human emotion. I've found that having a dog is the best ice-breaker in the world. When I take Angus for a walk I end up talking to so many fellow dog lovers because you have that common interest (and also because he's as cute as a button). You won't become bosom buddies with everyone you talk to, but at least it means you've connected with someone that day. If you don't have a dog of your own, why not offer to take a friend's for a walk? You'll both benefit from it. There are also apps and online services, like BorrowMyDoggy (www.borrowmydoggy.com) that can match you with a pooch that needs walking.

Having Angus means I never feel lonely now. If I want to get outside and meet new people then we head out on one of our long walks but he's also brilliant company if we're on our own. You can tell him anything and he always keeps a secret.

FOUNTAINS AND DRAINS

The best cure for a low mood is to help someone else feel better. In my job, it's very important to make people feel comfortable and to let them know that I care. And we all should do that! I've noticed that many people are drawn to those who are inquisitive and want to know how other people are. I always say that it's good to be interesting, but it's even better to be interested.

So be that person who brightens someone's day. My friend and former editor, Sue Walton, is one of those people who always makes me feel better. As soon as I set eyes on her cheery face, I feel instantly happier. Her genuine, caring nature and kindness mean she is much loved. We should all try to be more like her.

It's easy to take those closest to you for granted. Some people think their closest pals are hanging on a hook, and they can lift them on and off as they please, but everyone has a limit, so I've learned to be mindful of how much I'm giving and taking. If anything, I try to be especially considerate towards the friends that I know are the most forgiving.

Sometimes the people we love the most are the ones we take for granted because we think we can get away with it. I've learned to make time for the people I care about, because life can get in the way and you suddenly realise that you haven't seen or spoken to one or more of your good friends for several months. Even if you just give them a quick call to let them know you're thinking about them, or a text to keep the lines of communication open, it means so much.

You lose and gain friendships as you go through life. I think we all become more discerning about people; when you're at school you invite your whole class to your birthday party, even if you're not great pals, because that's how things are done. Then as you get older you naturally shed friends, whether it's down to geography or a change in circumstances, or just that you grow apart. And that's ok.

When you're young, you spread your net far and wide and everyone you meet becomes a friend, or a friend of a friend, but your circle becomes smaller once everyone becomes busy with careers and families, and eventually you're just left with your hardcore pals.

This reduced social circle can be hard to adjust to. We're taught to think we should be friends with everyone and that we're somehow a failure if we're not. However, it's healthy to know when a friendship has run its course. I've become much better at letting go of people who drag me down. I'm not talking about friends that are going through a bad time, I feel very honoured that I have friends who feel like they can phone me up any time and talk to me about whatever's bothering them. However, some people are always negative and miserable and seem to want everyone else, including you, to feel the same.

It's detrimental to be around a continuously negative person. Some people are fountains and some are drains. People who always have something to moan about and don't give you anything back are drains. We all know them; they're the people who can walk into a room and dampen the atmosphere in two seconds flat, and there comes a point where we have to say enough is enough. Talking to people that you love and who you know have your best interests at heart is a tonic. These fountains of love and energy are who we should choose to be around.

Signs that someone might be a drain:

- *You call to say 'I'm feeling rubbish' only for them to turn around and say, 'You're feeling rubbish? Wait until you hear about my day.' Competitive misery is unhealthy.*

- *They're always in transmit mode. They don't ask how you're doing, except as an afterthought. After speaking with them, you feel worse than you did before.*

- *They always think their glass is half empty, that everyone else is leading a better life and they are missing out. You'll try everything to cheer them up and you will exhaust yourself in the process, and actually they're secretly happy the way they are. You have a finite amount of energy, so spend it wisely.*

- *You see their name pop up on your phone and think, 'Oh no, I don't want to answer that.' This is a good indication that this person is not someone you want in your life. Sometimes you have to be ruthless for your own sake.*

- *The next time you have a conversation, take note of how many times they say 'I' and how many times they ask you questions about yourself. There'll always be times when your friend needs to talk about themselves more, but is it a common pattern in your friendship?*

HOW TO STEP AWAY

Some people are simply happy being unhappy, although of course, you do have to take into account whether this person has experienced trauma or has mental health problems. If that's the case, the kindest thing to do is direct them towards professional help. However, even if someone has perfectly understandable reasons for being a drain, you have to put your own wellbeing first.

If you've identified a drain, you don't necessarily have to end your friendship, sometimes it can be good just to be aware of a relationship's balance. I have a pal who is very negative for no good reason, and I always try to focus her mind on something positive, like a holiday she has coming up. I try to remind her of all the good things in her life. I like her, and she's worth the effort, but with some people you have to accept you are fighting a losing battle.

We only have a certain number of hours in our day, so why would we spend it with people who drain us? People tend not to know that they are drains; sometimes they aren't aware that they're just talking about themselves all the time.

If you have a drain in your life, you may even be feeding their misery by listening to and indulging their negativity. You don't have to fall out with them or decide you're never going to speak to them again. If you're brave enough, or the opportunity presents itself, you could even consider telling them, 'I know you've got problems and I care for you deeply, but I have to step away for a little while.' Stepping away can be the kindest thing for both of you, so keep that in the forefront of your mind if you do decide to reduce contact.

HELPING OTHERS THROUGH GRIEF AND LONELINESS

Losing your partner or going through a divorce are some of the toughest experiences in life – both are like having your heart ripped out of your body. When you've always had that person to turn to, their absence is a constant agony.

When someone's partner dies, everyone tends to flock to them for the first few weeks, or even months, but as time goes by, people slip away. It's our responsibility to check on them and see how they're doing, and make sure they're not sitting at home on their own feeling miserable. Starting again is hard, but sometimes people have no choice, and it's up to us to make that stage of someone's life a little easier.

In my opinion, you can't say the wrong thing, and even if you do, if you're saying it with the best intentions, people usually understand.

All anyone in this situation wants is for you to check in to see how they are and if they need help. Maybe offer to take some meals round to them, buy them a lovely book to read, or see if they want to go to the cinema so they can take some time out without having to talk. Even if there isn't anything you can do at that time, the very fact that you've offered will mean such a lot.

We now do most of our shopping online and sometimes there's no reason to leave the house at all, so making an effort to get some human contact is essential for someone who is suddenly on their own. Some elderly people don't talk to anyone for weeks on end. In the old days, if the milkman realised the bottles hadn't been taken in the neighbours would have been alerted that something was amiss and knocked on the door, but that doesn't happen anymore.

It's harder now that communities are scattered all over the place. I think some people worry about approaching others in case they're rebuffed, but saying hello to the elderly woman who lives in your block of flats might just make her day.

The internet can be a lifeline, because there are so many forums and ways for people to keep in touch. There are lots of classes around the country to teach people the ropes, too, but they need to know about them, and that's where the rest of us come in.

SEX, LOVE, MARRIAGE, RELATIONSHIPS

Relationships can be tricky, but being with the right person makes you light up. I definitely shine more brightly when I'm in Steve's company. I just have to look at him and he makes me smile, but like any other couple, we've had our ups and downs along the way.

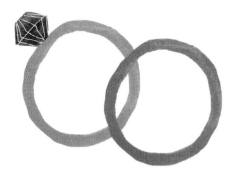

KICK-START YOUR RELATIONSHIP

Sometimes when the kids leave home, couples look at each other and ask, 'Who are you again?' This time in your life is the perfect opportunity to reignite your relationship.

At the beginning of a relationship, it's all excitement and fireworks, then children and jobs come along and doing fun things together gets pushed further and further down the list.

Everybody's relationship is different and it's something that every couple has to work at. A good marriage doesn't just happen; it's not all fairy tales and unicorns farting rainbows. A normal couple will argue about underpants on the floor or wet towels left in a heap, but even those annoying niggles, when set alongside fun times, add up to something special.

Steve and I married in 1992 and we have had our moments over the years, but he truly is one of the kindest and funniest men I've ever met. No one has a bad word to say about him. He's upfront, kind, loyal and my very best friend. He tells me off when he needs to, especially when I'm worrying about something I have no power to change or fix, but he's also my staunchest ally and defender.

Steve makes me laugh more than anyone I know, and being able to have fun in a relationship keeps things light-hearted, even during the tougher times. One running joke that's managed to last our entire marriage is our monkey gag. It's so daft but somehow it's stood the test of time.

It goes like this . . . Steve will say to me, 'There's a lovely photo of you on page 17 of the newspaper today.' Then when I turn to page 17 there will be a particularly unflattering photo of a chimp or some kind of monkey. Or he will say, 'You are on BBC2 right now' and it will be a wildlife film about baboons. It still makes me laugh even after all these years and I am just as cheeky to him.

If your relationship is stuck in a rut, there are a lot of things you can do to make it better. For a start, you have to talk to each other and be honest about how you're feeling. It's a hard conversation to have, but it's vital. You need to find out if there's still enough love and shared experience there to make it salvageable.

Some relationships can be mended, even if things feel as if they are at breaking point. Life isn't like the movies and you don't live happily ever after with no effort from either side. You need to be upfront about the things that annoy you about each other and work on them before the situation turns toxic.

People sometimes ditch their partner purely because they think they can do better and the grass is greener. Before that happens, take a breath and at least give it your best shot. If that doesn't work, then you can walk away knowing you tried everything. People can give up on relationships too easily, but on the flip side if you don't think there's anything left, you can't keep fighting a losing battle. You deserve to be happy and it's better to part ways while you still have some good memories.

In any relationship, it's easy to get stuck in a rut. You can have as many restarts as you want, but you have to make them happen. You can't sit and wait for the man or woman of your dreams to come to you. You need to make an effort and find your passions.

If you're single and you want to meet someone new, you have nothing to lose by trying a dating app or website. I know it takes courage but there are some incredible success stories. Two of my best friends met their partners online. They didn't end up with the first guys they met and they had to kiss a few frogs first, but they ended up meeting terrific men and they are all very happy. My advice would be to have fun, but be safe. Don't go to someone's house on the first date. My friends always gave me the details of any new man they were meeting, and where they were going. They met first in a public place, and only progressed when there was trust established.

It goes without saying that if a relationship is abusive in any way, you need to get out as quickly as you can. There is support out there – womensaid.org.uk, refuge.org.uk and relate.org.uk are just a few of the brilliant places that offer help – and you need to know that you are not alone and that you are worth so much more. Talk to a friend or family member you trust and get help. There is always a way. Do not put up with abuse.

DATE NIGHT

Most of us know that a weekly, fortnightly or, at a stretch, monthly 'date night' makes all the difference in the world, but hardly anyone I know puts that rule into practice. Don't let life get in the way of your relationship.

A date needn't be a meal at a swanky, expensive restaurant. In fact, if you're trying to reignite a relationship, I think that can feel a bit intimidating and contrived. What's more important is being able to make a genuine connection with your partner so your favourite local bistro or pub is fine. If you're really busy, you could even just plan a night at home together. Get the best china out, light some candles, turn the TV off, put the phones away and talk to each other!

EXERCISE

Make a list of date ideas here so that you have
no excuse to put it off!

_____

_____

_____

_____

_____

_____

_____

_____

_____

_____

LET'S TALK ABOUT SEX

There are three things our children should be learning about at school: how to cook, how to pay the bills and, of course, what sex is all about.

We shouldn't be embarrassed about sex and we need to ensure that children have the facts and that they know how to protect themselves against becoming pregnant or contracting sexually transmitted diseases.

We need to make sure that we can talk to our children about sex and keep those vital lines of communication open. It's important to stress that no one, boy or girl, man or woman, should feel pressurised into doing anything they aren't comfortable with.

Sex shouldn't be about perfectly toned bodies and multiple orgasms, but that's what you see in so many explicit TV shows and movies. You should take your time, talking, exploring and finding out what works. You should be able to have open conversations about what you like and don't like. We should all be fulfilled and contented, and if we don't enjoy what someone is doing we should be able to tell them.

People seem to have forgotten that sex is not just an expression of love, it's also good fun. It's as normal as eating and sleeping in adult life. That's what a good relationship is about. Sex is still all a bit 'nudge nudge, wink wink' in this country, but it's not something we should be shy or embarrassed about. On the flip side, we don't want to go the other way and treat it as if it doesn't mean anything at all and is just like blowing your nose.

Don't you think that 'wooing' has gone out of the window? Just the basic getting to know someone before you jump into bed has all but disappeared. Porn is so readily available now and I really worry that young women in particular are being coerced into doing things they don't want to do, and I am genuinely concerned that people may lose the intimacy of sex.

I must admit I haven't seen much porn, but I've had to watch some explicit content when we've covered certain topics on the show and in my capacity as an agony aunt, and I've been shocked and saddened as well as angered by it.

I've seen enough to know that the women in the videos are completely unrealistic and it's putting terrible pressure on young men and women. I really hate the way women are depicted in porn, and even in some music videos, and I fear that young men think that's how their girlfriends should behave or should even be treated.

Obviously we weren't exposed to porn like this when I was growing up. The only porn available was tucked away on the top shelf of the magazine rack in petrol stations. We were pretty innocent and we had to fumble our way through together, and hope we eventually got there. We didn't have anything to compare ourselves to, which was a blessing, whereas young girls today are comparing themselves to these female porn stars with pneumatic false boobs and no body hair.

That loss of discovering what sex is all about together as a couple is terribly sad, as is the loss of innocence amongst younger and younger children. We need to protect them by using web filters and parental controls that are offered via broadband providers, and letting them know that what is out there online is not reality.

It's brilliant that there are programmes that talk about sex, and that young people can learn from them, and if it is done with a sense of humour, that's great. However, the barriers are being pushed and pushed and I worry about where it's going to end up.

I do think that some TV shows are putting out the wrong message. Some young men and women on reality shows are having actual sex on TV with multiple partners and genuinely don't seem to think there's anything wrong with that. I'm flabbergasted by how normalised that has become in such a short space of time.

To me, sex is such a private and special thing and I don't understand young men and women having so little respect for themselves, especially when they know their behaviour influences others. If you don't have respect for yourself, what have you got? Fans of these shows even make their own sex tapes in the mistaken belief they are being edgy and cool.

I'm far from being a prude, but once those explicit photos and videos are out there, there's no taking them back, and they may well regret it when they are older. The trend of sending semi-naked or naked pictures of yourself to other people appals me, too. If someone puts that online, or even if you do, you cannot erase it from the internet. Once it's been shared the genie's out of the bottle.

It may seem fine when you're a teenager, but what happens when you are applying for a job, or when you grow up and have children? It doesn't bear thinking about. That stuff isn't going anywhere, so we have a responsibility to our kids to help them navigate their way through it. When the time is right we need to sit them down and have a proper chat about the effect that posting naked or explicit images can have on their future. We can't shy away from that stuff, or get embarrassed.

I don't care if it sounds preachy or old-fashioned, but young people need to value themselves more. You *have* to value yourself or no one else is going to. I'm not suggesting for a second that we go backwards to a time when women were supposed to be virgins before they were wed, or unmarried mothers were made to feel ashamed – that would be ludicrous – but I do think that if you have sex with someone it should be your choice, and on your terms, and it should make you feel good.

Sometimes you might just be scratching an itch, and that's fine because it's your body, and if you want to have sex, good luck to you, but it shouldn't be something you feel obliged or pressurised to do. You deserve better than that.

FAMILY

There is no such thing as the 'perfect' family. Each has its own quirks and complications, but that's what makes it so special. I've learned some of my biggest lessons from my family, and becoming a mum changed me more than anything.

MOTHERHOOD ISN'T ONE-SIZE-FITS-ALL

You can read all the books in the world and watch every TV show going, but the only thing that truly teaches you about motherhood is holding a tiny baby in your arms and having to just get on with it.

There is so much information out there for new mums it can make your head spin. When Rosie was small I soaked up advice from those closest to me and followed all the sensible health and safety guidelines, but ultimately I trusted my instincts and did what felt right.

I've had times when I've questioned whether I've done the right thing with Rosie, and I'm sure I've made mistakes along the way, but all we can do is our best. Everything I did, and continue to do, I believe, is in Rosie's best interests.

We're all finding our way as we go along. It's a bit like starting a new job and being expected to know everything on your first day. You have to hit the ground running because that little one isn't going to give you time to settle in or wait until you've perfected the art of changing a crying baby's nappy after just two hours' sleep.

Like everything, you get better at being a mum with practice, and you only learn what works and what doesn't by trying it. Some mums find they can nap when their baby naps, and some women find it makes them feel even more tired. You'll work out what suits you.

Don't beat yourself up if you don't do every single thing the 'right' way. Unless your toddler is wrecking the house and running amok, let them have fun. It doesn't matter if your house isn't perfect, the Tidy Police don't actually exist, and if anyone judges you for having a living room full of toys and a massive ironing basket, they aren't worth bothering about.

A plea from the heart to modern parents: don't stick your kids in front of the TV or iPad for hours on end and use it as a babysitter, and *please* take notice of them. It drives me mad when I see parents out glued to their phones and ignoring the children. Put down your phone and talk to your child. Children are like little sponges, soaking up information and knowledge, and they are an endless source of joy because they are so curious about the world. They will ask you impossible questions and they actually believe that you know the answer to everything.

It's so important to make sure you read your child a bedtime story, too, and encourage them to read books themselves when they are older. A love of reading was one of the best gifts my parents ever gave me, and it has enriched my life, and reading together every night provides a routine and something that you can both look forward to.

Our children grow up so fast, and you don't want to regret that you didn't spend enough time with them because you were too busy answering emails or looking at the latest nonsense on Twitter. When Rod Stewart came on my show he admitted that he missed his older kids growing up because he was working so hard to provide for them. He said he was so lucky that he got a second chance with his wife Penny and their two boys because now he's able to play football and hang out with them and watch them grow up. He's lucky that he got that second chance because a lot of people don't.

While you want to give your child attention and encourage them to express themselves, please don't feel you can't tell your child off. A spoilt brat is a nightmare and I cannot abide seeing badly behaved children in restaurants or on public transport being allowed to scream, shout and generally be a complete pain in the bum. Children won't be well behaved all the time and they will test you, but stay strong!

Children need boundaries and they need to be taught consideration for others. They should also be encouraged to amuse themselves when you need to get things done, but it's all about balance. You don't have to give them your undivided attention at all times, but equally don't just give your children 'stuff' and then not engage with them.

My brother used to drive me mad when he was a kid because it was 'Why, why, why, why?' to everything. But looking back on it now, I think it was wonderful that he was so curious. The day your kids stop asking you 'Why?' is quite sad, because it means they've started finding things out on their own and they don't need you as much.

We gave Rosie a lot of attention, but we also let her sit and read a book on her own. Kids need their space, too, and they don't always have to be doing things and be in every club going. I actually think it's really important to let them be a bit bored, because that's when they start to use their imagination.

It was also so important for Steve and me to teach Rosie good manners. It might sound old-fashioned, but being considerate and kind will make your child endearing, likeable and happier as a result.

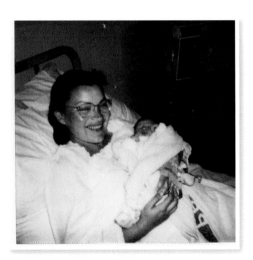 

EXERCISE

What do you think are the three most important qualities to pass on to your children? How might you help your children build these attributes?

_____

_____

_____

_____

_____

_____

_____

_____

BECOMING A MUM MADE ME BETTER AT MY JOB

I absolutely think being a mother made me better at my job. I wasn't particularly self-centred before I had Rosie, but having someone else to think about made me even less so. When you have a baby your focus shifts. It's not all about you anymore. You see the bigger picture and you have far more empathy.

I became a more patient and understanding interviewer. I really thought deeply about the people I was speaking to and tried to walk in their shoes, especially if they had a tough and emotional story to tell.

I think being a mum makes you grow up and become far more caring and considerate. I am now always that woman who has a spare hanky or plaster in her handbag or a hug for someone who needs it. Motherhood made me less selfish and much more capable of helping others around me, particularly in the workplace. I became a real team player and far more supportive of everyone who worked with me on the show, especially those who need a bit of extra help.

Over the past 25 years since Rosie was born that has become a way of life, and something I always try to pass on.

Some people say that when you have a baby your world becomes smaller, but I think it becomes larger because you start to look at the bigger picture. You realise that important issues like crime or climate change directly affect your child's future. They are real problems, not abstract concepts. You want to make the world a better and safer place for your precious baby.

Work/life balance can be hard, and certainly in our 20s and 30s it's easy to become obsessed with work and think it's the most important thing in the world. I got better at redressing the balance when I had Rosie. Not surprisingly, as a working mother I suffered from terrible 'mum guilt' at times. Because of the nature of his job, as a freelance cameraman, Steve was around a lot more than most dads and did a lot with Rosie. I was so lucky that Steve was a very hands-on dad from the word go – he gave Rosie her first bath when I was scared I'd drop her. I actually spent the entire first few weeks wandering around in a daze wearing an old tartan dressing gown with bits of toast in my hair.

As I was working unconventional hours, I couldn't take Rosie to school in the morning (I would have had to leave her at the gate at 5am – not ideal), but I tried to pick her up as often as I possibly could. No one ever questioned Steve when he worked late or had to go away, but there were times when I felt that people judged me a bit for having a career *and* a child. Sadly, there are still hurdles to overcome when it comes to equality, but with the introduction of shared parental leave I do think we're making progress.

Rosie would sometimes think my job was pretty cool if she got to meet Westlife or Blue, but other than that me being on TV was just normal for her. I'd leave my job behind when I got home and I was just her mum, and I definitely don't live in a celebrity bubble. Steve and I had both agreed that we wanted to bring her up in a stable, ordinary environment.

TEEN SPIRIT

I learned not to take it personally if I ended up in the firing line when Rosie was a teenager; like all teens, she had her moments and sometimes she just needed to vent.

I talked to Rosie a lot while she was growing up and it was so important to me to keep those lines of communication open. She talked to her friends about things that she wouldn't speak to me about, and I think that's totally healthy. I made a conscious effort to always let Rosie know she could come to me if she wanted to talk, but I never smothered her. If ever I was worried about her I would ask if she was ok, but I would leave it up to her to decide how much she wanted to share.

Rosie and I have a really strong relationship but I've always given her her own space. I know Fergie, the Duchess of York, used to regularly go out clubbing with her daughters when they were younger, and I don't get that *at all*. I always say that I'm not Rosie's friend, I'm her mum. She's got pals to talk to, but I'm always there when she needs me and she knows I'm always in her corner.

Teenagers rebel, and quite right too. I was a nightmare for my mum when I was about 15 or 16; we argued all the time and there was a lot of door slamming (me, not my mum!). Teenagers should be given a bit of free rein to rebel without being utterly obnoxious and objectionable. You *should* think you can change the world at that age. That's the time when you're often angry and want to stand up for what you believe in because you're discovering what matters to you.

Teenagers should also go on demonstrations and speak out against things they're passionate about; it's the only way to bring about change. I understand why they think our government are 'a bunch of feckers', because they're having to live through a shambolic period of political turmoil. I think they've got a right to be angry. I am too. We deserve better from all of our politicians right across the spectrum. They have been miserable failures, and British politics has become horribly toxic.

I admire the way school kids in the USA are demanding gun control and young people across the globe are taking to the streets for action on climate change. I just hope those in power are listening. This generation are the ones who will be voting soon so that they *can* bring about change.

There's so much going on in the world it's impossible for us to throw our weight behind every campaign, but it's important to stand up for what you believe in. If there's something you're really passionate about I would wholeheartedly encourage you to 'do your bit'. It's only by putting our hands up and being seen that we can make a difference. Even if it's just signing a petition, taking part in a march or doing some fundraising for a cause close to your heart, those little actions can add up to something huge.

Being a part of something positive will make you feel uplifted and empowered. We may not be teens anymore, but that doesn't mean we can't share their incredible hunger for making a difference.

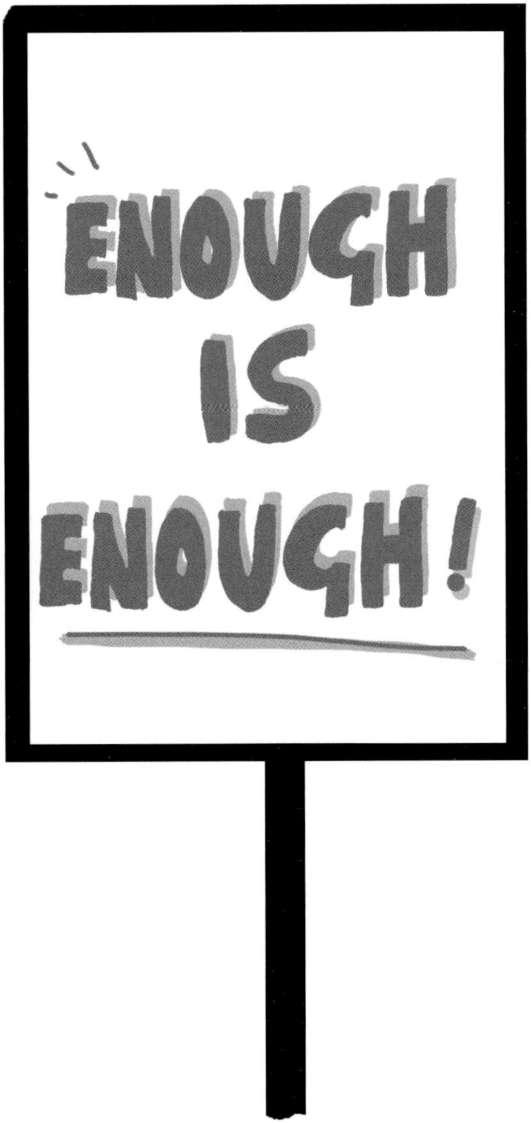
ENOUGH
IS
ENOUGH!

EXERCISE

Which causes were you most passionate about as a teenager? Do you feel the same way now? Pick one cause or charity and make a pledge to yourself to help it in some way every month.

I promise I will . . .

_____

_____

_____

_____

_____

_____

_____

_____

EMPTY NEST SYNDROME

Empty nest syndrome is real and it's tough to go through.

I brought my daughter up to be an independent woman, then she left home to go to university and I missed her so much. I had brought her up to paddle her own canoe, but that didn't mean I wasn't sad to see her go.

It actually begins years before, when they go to nursery school, start discovering new interests and making new friends. Anyone who says the first day of school isn't hard is a total liar. I can't imagine a mum or dad that didn't sob when their little one walked into the playground on their own. Even though you know it's a perfectly normal part of them growing up and developing, you feel a sense of sadness and even loss that you aren't the centre of their world anymore.

I think most of us find it difficult to adjust when our children leave home, but we know they have to live their own lives. You have to let them fly. Rosie will always have a bedroom wherever Steve and I are, no matter how old she is. She might only come back from Singapore once or twice a year, but everything is still there for her, and I go in and dust it every week and have a bit of an imaginary chat with her.

There's a fine line between caring for your kids and smothering them. You can't expect them to phone you every hour of the day, but they should know that you're on hand to help if they need you. I'm 60 and my mum and dad still worry about me, and they always will. That's what happens when you are a parent! Luckily, it's so easy to keep in touch these days. My mum regularly pings me a message about something on the show (she watches every morning and is a highly valuable critic) and I keep in touch regularly with visits, phone calls and also online. Despite the geographical distance between us, Rosie and I message and chat to each other on WhatsApp a lot, but I don't want her to feel like that's a duty. I do want our contact to be something she enjoys rather than a chore. That's when technology and social media is at its best; it can make such a difference to families who live far away from each other.

Each stage of a child's life is so different, whether they're starting school or getting their first Saturday job or leaving home, you feel everything so deeply on their behalf. You have to deal with each new stage at a time and try not to jump forward too much, and it's so important to keep an open mind as they start to make their own decisions, too. You may not always approve of their choice of friends, partner or career path, but you can't dictate your opinions to your children. You have to allow them to make their mistakes.

As soon as you decide to have a baby, you've got a job for life, and sometimes you will need to put your own feelings and wishes aside and make sacrifices for them.

HOME

I love to travel, but few things make me happier than returning to the warmth and comfort of my home. I'm sure you'll agree there's something deeply satisfying about having all your personal things around you. When I'm sitting on my sofa with a cup of tea and a book, everything feels right with the world.

HOME IS WHERE MY HEART IS

I think because I've been freelance for so many years and don't have the security of a stable job (I know have been on breakfast TV for over 35 years, but it's a brutal industry and you are only as good as your viewing figures), I like other things in my life to be settled.

Everything in my house is tidy. If you open my kitchen cupboards all the labels on the tins will be facing the same way and my clothes are hung up by colour, and obviously, like Joan Crawford, There Are No Wire Hangers. Ever!

I like everything to be in order. I can't relax properly if anything's out of place. If I see something that needs doing out of the corner of my eye, even if it's a book that needs straightening, I have to get up and do it. In fact, I can be a bit too anal about orderliness. I was doing a yoga class recently and we were all supposed to be concentrating on our poses, but I could see that the door of the water fridge in the studio wasn't closed properly and it was *all* I could think about. Everyone else was 'ohm-ing' away and looking really chilled out and I had to get up and shut the bloody door.

I have to consciously allow myself to let go of this striving for perfection and remind myself that the world isn't going to end if a picture frame is wonky. I have a word with myself when I get a bit too tidy and controlling. I say to myself, are people going to come into my bathroom and give me marks out of ten for cleanliness like an episode of *Four In A Bed*? What's the worst that can happen? They won't visit again?

Your home isn't for show, and although I'm tidy, my house is full of clutter and has lots of character. I need to remember that it's ok to be little messy sometimes. Clean, of course, but messy is perfectly fine.

It's impossible to be precious and house proud when you have kids, and I had no choice but to live with chaos when Rosie was growing up because she needed to be able to play with her toys. I had a basket in the corner of the living room, and at the end of each day when she went to bed I would chuck all her toys and dollies in there until the following day. I do the same with Angus and his chew toys now. Having him is like having a toddler that will never grow up, which is partly why I love him so much.

Even though I like things to be in order, my home is very personal and cosy. I'm not minimalist and I've accumulated a lot of stuff, but I feel that I've got reasons for my clutter. I find it very weird when you go into someone's kitchen and it looks like they've never cooked a meal in it. I love a home that's lived in, with fridge magnets from the places you've visited and kids' drawings stuck up on the walls.

I still have everything Rosie made for me when she was a child and I will never, ever throw them away. I have ticket stubs and entry passes around my mirror, and sometimes when I'm brushing my hair I'll see a ticket for a show and remember what a great time I had that night.

I do the same with photographs. I like them so much better than ornaments and I have framed photos everywhere. Every one of them tells a story. I have pictures of my mum, Rosie and myself at the same age framed next to each other, and I love looking at them. Your home should reflect who you are and it should be comfortable.

I don't judge people when I go into their houses (although I do find it baffling if they don't have any books) and I hope people don't judge me on mine. If someone is going to come in and evaluate everything, I don't want them in my house anyway!

So here are my top tips for a calm and cheerful home:

- *Put your favourite photo by your front door. I have a photo of me in Antarctica with a waddle of penguins (that's the collective name for penguins on land. When they are in the sea it's a 'raft') by my front door, and every time I leave the house it makes me smile.*

- *Books, books, and more books. You can never have too many. I love being surrounded by paperbacks and hardbacks; it reminds me of how much there is out there in the world to discover. I keep big coffee-table books that can transport me to another world in my living room. One is full of photos of Bali, because I love it there, and the other one is about Antarctica, which, you might have gathered, I'm obsessed with.*

- *Plants dotted throughout the home create a feeling of calm and clean the air, too.*

- *Scent really sets the tone of your home. I love a diffuser or a scented candle. Nothing too artificial – my favourites are geranium, lavender or roses.*

- *Fresh flowers can make all the difference to a room, even if it's just a bunch of daffodils for £1. I put them all around the house in springtime in every available vase and old jam jars.*

- *Scatter cushions should be all over the house. You can never have too many. I think it's a girl thing.*

CLEAR YOUR HOUSE TO CLEAR YOUR MIND

There is nothing quite like that feeling when you've gone through all your cupboards and had a good clear-out. It's satisfying, even cleansing, and it's a lovely warm feeling knowing that if you give your unwanted clothes and jumble to charity, someone else is going to get the chance to enjoy them.

Everything you have around you should make you feel happy, or, as Japanese tidying guru Marie Kondo says, 'spark joy'. Don't keep things out of guilt because they were expensive or a gift. It's easy to feel a bit uncomfortable when you give things away if you don't think you've worn or used them enough, but set that 'stuff' free! It's only going to clog up your house. The objects we surround ourselves with can help us to stay in a positive frame of mind.

Do yourself and the environment a favour by recycling, and know that someone else is going to get the benefit of the things you no longer want. I'm ruthless when I have a clear-out, and nothing makes me happier than seeing a big pile of clothes destined for the charity shop.

I know having a sort-out can feel a bit overwhelming, so break it up into manageable chunks. Allocate a day to each room and work your way through it a bit at a time. If you haven't used something for six months or worn clothes for over a year, the chances are you don't need it anymore. If you're not sure you can bear to part with something just yet, give yourself a grace period

by storing it. Package up the stuff you 'may' want and store it for six months. If you don't think about it or miss it, it's got to go.

THE POWER OF ANIMALS

Pets are incredible, and they can make most people feel instantly better. When my Granny Kelly was 91, she went into a care home because she was suffering from dementia. One week, I went to visit and brought our dog with us and I swear the whole place lit up. You would not believe the difference that little border terrier made to the atmosphere in the room. It brought so much joy to everyone and I saw people come alive, with big smiles on their faces.

Ricky Gervais is a real softie when it comes to animals, and when he came on my show to talk about his series *After Life* he brought along the beautiful German shepherd that appeared in the show with him. He talked about how having to look after the dog was what saved his character after the death of his wife. Having to get up and make sure the dog was fed and walked each day brought him back from the brink of suicide. I'm sure that happens in real life, too. In fact, studies have shown that people who have pets are fitter and more sociable, and having a pet can even help to lower anxiety levels.

Animals can bring such comfort and I'm sure they instinctively know when we need support. When Steve and I went hiking in Uganda there was a man in our small group who had a brain tumour. The trip was part of his bucket list, and although he struggled through the rough terrain, you could tell he was loving every second. As we were walking we stumbled upon a beautiful female gorilla. We all sat down and bowed our heads, so that she wouldn't be frightened and run off. She immediately went over to this man, reached out her hand and put it on his head. It was one of the most moving things I've ever seen and the man was so overwhelmed he started crying. Actually, we were all crying. It was as though that intelligent, empathetic gorilla knew that he needed some extra care.

My brother suffers from asthma, so the only pets I had growing up were two goldfish called Pinky and Perky. My mum was never a dog or cat lover, but when Steve and I got our first border terrier, Rocky, she absolutely adored him, and she adores Angus, too.

I was devastated when Rocky died from cancer aged 11, and I wasn't ready to get another dog immediately because I had to mourn him. He was a big part of our family. We missed him so much and it was never a case of trying to replace him. We *couldn't* have replaced him. Some people think a dog is just 'a dog', or a cat is just 'a cat', but they're individuals, just like people. They've all got their own personalities and funny little ways, and no two are the same.

Steve and I really missed having a dog around, though, so 18 months after Rocky died, when Rosie moved to Singapore, we felt the time was right to get another one and I put out some feelers. After a while, we got a call from a breeder saying that they had a male border terrier puppy available.

Rosie was coming home for Christmas and I wanted to surprise her, so I kept Angus a secret. When we brought him home, she thought I was holding a stuffed toy (I had put him in a cute and very cosy reindeer outfit). Then I turned him around and when she realised it was a real puppy she was beyond excited. It was such a gorgeous moment.

Angus has brought so much joy into our lives and he is our priority when it comes to scheduling and holidays. Dogs are a joy but they are hard work, and people sometimes forget that. They don't fit into all lifestyles and you can't leave them alone for hours at a time, they need a routine and a stable, loving home. They are not just to be taken out only at weekends or carried around in handbags, either, and it upsets me so much when people get dogs as accessories; they are living creatures with wants and needs. They are not toys, and although we bought Angus at Christmas we know that he is with us for life, and we love to take good care of him.

Dog owners are usually a highly responsible bunch, but when an animal attacks or misbehaves we are looking at the wrong end of the leash. We need to love our animals but we also have a duty to train them properly and be considerate to others. Allowing your dog to foul the pavement or countryside is unforgivable and it drives me nuts when people pick up after their dog and then take the poo bag and hang it in a tree. I know it's not much fun carrying it around until you come across a bin, but it's much better than leaving it dangling off a bush for someone else to deal with. It's disgusting and harmful.

I feel so strongly about how we must all respect the environment and do our bit. We are all responsible for the world we live in and it drives me up the wall that people can't pick up their rubbish and take it with them. If we don't change our attitudes we are going to end up buried in litter. When I see people chucking rubbish onto the pavement out of their car, I can only think, 'What is your house like?'

We've seen how animals and marine life all over the world are getting killed and injured by plastic. When you go for a walk in a beauty spot and it's filled with litter, it's soul-destroying. I was up in the Outer Hebrides walking on a beautiful beach recently and there was so much rubbish coming in with the tide it made me want to cry, and then it made me angry. I got a big (recyclable) bag and cleared it up and I felt so much better afterwards. We shouldn't have to clear up after each other; it all starts with you not throwing your crisp packet onto the street.

Of course, it's not always practical to be completely plastic-free, but I do try to use far less. Don't think 'I can't do anything about it', we can *all* do something to help the planet, no matter how small. It may feel insignificant but it will have an impact; we can make the world a better, cleaner place one sweetie wrapper at a time. We should all do what we can and show some respect to this amazing planet of ours, and teach our children to do the same.

Some easy ways you can help the environment:

- *Use refillable coffee cups and water bottles.*

- *Unplug electricals when you're not using them.*

- *Use eco-friendly cleaning products as often as you can.*

- *Always use reusable bags. Plastic bags are a big no-no.*

- *Take part in a community litter clear-up (check out local groups on Facebook for upcoming ones).*

- *Get involved in a tree planting programme.*

- *Support local wildlife by putting a bird box or hedgehog home in your garden. See www.wildlifetrusts.org or www.rspb.co.uk for loads more great ideas.*

- *Collect rainwater and use it to water your garden.*

- *Recycle, recycle, recycle.*

- *Always put your rubbish in a bin when you're out and about. There is no excuse!*

PURPOSE

Discovering what makes our hearts sing is crucial if we want to feel fulfilled. Whether it's a job we love, a great relationship or even rewarding hobbies, doing what you love each day will make you dazzle.

THE TIME IS NOW!

It's easy to get stuck in a rut, but there is no rule that says you have to do the same thing for ever and ever. You can have as many restarts as you want, but YOU have to make them happen. You can't sit and wait for the world to come to you. You need to get up and find what makes you shine.

We can become more timid and play it safe as we get older, but I think we should do the opposite. I definitely still push myself, but I am well aware that I'm lucky enough to be in a job that I find fascinating, interesting and stimulating.

Get out of your comfort zone; you don't want to be 75 and think, 'I wish I'd changed jobs when I was younger instead of spending years doing something I didn't enjoy.' You can change your life in a moment.

Maybe you want to write a book? Self-publishing makes that possible nowadays. Or perhaps you want to learn how to paint? Why not join an art class? The only thing holding you back is you.

If you are not enjoying your job, don't wait until you're completely depressed to start looking around for different opportunities. If you're not ready to make that leap, talk to your boss or HR department and see if the things that are bothering you about your job can be remedied. Don't stay anywhere that is making you ill or miserable, but do wait until you have a new job in the bag before walking away from your current one.

You've only got one life and if you've always wanted to be a teacher, go and retrain. Or if you dream of setting up your own business, there is a great deal of advice online to help you do that. Just make sure you're coming from a solid grounding and be aware of the financial implications of your decision. It's great to be brave, but don't jump in (or out!) too quickly or without doing a bit of research first.

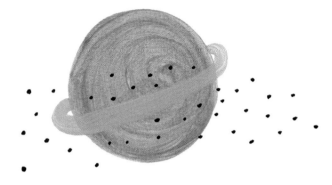

EXERCISE

What do you want to be when you grow up? Aspirations aren't just for children. I wanted to be an astronaut and I still do. Obviously, I'll never get that job, but I've read everything I can get my hands on about space and have been lucky enough to interview real-life spacemen, including our very own Tim Peake.

When I grow up I want to be a . . .

_____

_____

_____

_____

_____

_____

_____

_____

HARD AND RESILIENCE

My mum and dad were grafters and they instilled a real work ethic in me and my brother Graham, who is six years younger than me. That work ethic has stayed with me; sometimes I may even work too hard because of it, but I am getting better at taking a step back if I need to. Sort of.

I always wanted to pay my own way. When I was 14 I applied for a special under-16s work permit so I could earn a bit of extra pocket money. I got a Saturday job in Chelsea Girl, which was a cool clothes shop to work in back then. My uniform was made up of a brown A-line skirt and a white blouse covered in cherries, complete with a massive pointed collar and puffed sleeves. I thought I looked amazing. To be fair, this was in the 70s, possibly the least stylish decade in history, so my outfit wasn't as bad as it sounds.

I worked from midday until 4pm, mainly tidying rails of clothes, and was paid a whole pound for my shift. That sounds like nothing, but back then 25p an hour was a good wage for a girl of my age, and I was so proud of my first pay packet because I'd earned that money myself. Working hard and knowing you deserve the rewards is so satisfying.

It's also ok to fail. I've had moments where I've felt like my whole life was crumbling, but my worst experiences have always led to my best. I take inspiration from sports people; they have the most incredible focus and unshakable inner confidence. I'm not sure if that's down to training or their personality type, but I admire their resilience. If they get second place they won't let that inner confidence wobble and they won't berate themselves. They'll pick themselves up and they'll focus on getting gold next time.

But here's an idea: give yourself a pat on the back whether you come first or not.

Often it takes people on the outside to tell us what a good job we're doing, or show us how hard we're working, but we need to big ourselves up more often. We should recognise our own good qualities and congratulate ourselves on them rather than focusing on the things we want to change and trying to be 'better' all the time. I'm all for self-development and I will never stop learning and evolving, but I also take notice of the things I do well and the things I like about myself. That's key to feeling happy, so give yourself a big high five for all the brilliant things you do.

If I hadn't discovered I had the ability to pick myself up and soldier on, I absolutely would not be doing the job that I do today.

When I was 17, I was offered a place at university to study Russian and English. It was a very big deal; I would have been the first person in either the Kelly or McMahon family to go to university. I was all set to go, but then I saw an advert for a junior reporter role in our local newspaper and, suddenly, I knew that was what I wanted to do with my life. My parents didn't say anything at the time but I found out later that they were very disappointed I didn't take up that university offer. Back then, an important measure of your success as a parent was a photo on the mantelpiece of your child clutching a degree while wearing a black robe and a funny hat. My parents didn't discourage me in my career choice, but I know they were very worried.

I landed the job and did anything and everything that was asked of me. I got noticed by having the attitude of nothing was too much trouble. I remember volunteering to cover the dullest council meetings and to judge Bonny Baby competitions, and I reviewed local bands in my spare time. Eventually I was given my own column. It was a steep learning curve and I had some brilliant journalists teaching me, including Mike Barr, who taught me the joys of red wine as well as how to write a good intro to a lead story.

In those days there was no internet or mobile phones, so you had to go out and get the story, usually by meeting people in the local café or pub. Then you would get back to the office to write it up using actual paper and a typewriter. I miss the clacking noise of those keys, and the smell of printing ink takes me right back to the early '80s.

After five years on the paper, I was ready for a change and I contacted the BBC. I basically applied for every position going – I even applied to be a farming correspondent for the BBC. I didn't know one end of a cow from another, but I was willing to learn.

Back then you had to go and sit in front of a board of people when you were interviewed for a job at the Beeb. I reckoned if I kept popping up, eventually I would wear them down and they would cave in and say 'for goodness' sake, let's just give this girl a job'. My tactic worked. After numerous interviews I got a job as a researcher on a new show that was coming out called *60 Minutes*. It was an ill-fated programme, and didn't last very long, but it gave me my first break in TV.

When I joined the BBC my pay got cut in half, which wasn't ideal as I'd just bought a tiny flat in Glasgow with a massive mortgage. As a result, I had to get a second job as a waitress working evenings and weekends to pay my bills. I was the worst waitress in Glasgow, but it was a means to an end.

Right from the start, the BBC sent me out to film vox pops, where you stop people in the street to ask them random questions. My bosses would say to me, 'People like talking to you, Lorraine,' and off I would go to ask the unsuspecting, patient people of Glasgow a daft question. My ultimate plan was to become an onscreen news reporter, but in the meantime I'd ask people what they thought of the latest political scandal, or whether they reckoned the trend for ra-ra skirts was here to stay.

My next role was as a researcher on a couple of documentaries for a show called *Focal Point* (which us journos obviously renamed 'F***-all Point'). It was a tough job, but I learned from the best in the business, including the legendary late journalist who fronted the series, David Scott. I knew that ultimately I wanted to be doing his job.

One day, in 1984, the big boss of news called me into his office for a chat about my future. I knew there were a couple of TV reporter jobs up for grabs, which meant I'd get to do serious research and be in front of the camera. 'This is it!' I thought to myself. '*This* is my big moment.'

I stood in front of my boss in a freshly ironed shirt and a smart skirt feeling a mixture of nerves and excitement. I was already imagining making the phone call to my parents to tell them my great news. Then my boss pushed his glasses down his nose, looked me dead in the eye and said, 'You're never going to make it. No one on television speaks like you. You can get elocution lessons and try your luck somewhere else if you want to, but as for your future on air here? You've got no chance.' I came out of that meeting so downcast and crestfallen. My confidence was shattered.

At that point, things could have gone either way. I had a choice: I could believe that my boss was right and accept that I was never going to make it in my chosen field, or I could think, 'Sod it, I'm going to do it anyway.' I chose the latter. That toe-curling moment in my boss's office ended up being a blessing. I had to shake things up and believe in myself more than ever if I wanted to move on with my career.

Shortly afterwards, I heard through the grapevine that London-based *TV-am* were looking for a Scottish correspondent. *TV-am* wasn't doing very well at the time; in fact, it was on its last legs. They had hired a puppet called Roland Rat (cue all the jokes about a rat *joining* a sinking ship), but it was new, groundbreaking, raw telly, and *I wanted that job*.

Thanks to the confidence of youth, I went straight to the boss at *TV-am*, who invited me down to London for an interview. I would never have the nerve to do that now, but I was much more fearless back then. I guess I felt I had nothing to lose.

I did an audition for the boss, Bruce Gyngell. Bruce was a one-off. He loved the colour pink, did interviews with the broadsheets while bouncing on a trampoline in his office, and encouraged all his staff to have colonic irrigations and shiatsu massages!

When Bruce called to offer me the job, the words of my old boss at the BBC were playing on my mind so I said to Bruce, 'What about my accent? Is it going to be ok?' 'Well you sound Scottish and we want a Scottish correspondent, so what are you worried about?' he replied. That was me told.

It was a terrifying, exciting and demanding job, covering all the top stories in Scotland, coming live from the tiny studio in Glasgow, finding guests, writing briefs and organising the crew.

After covering the Lockerbie bombing in December 1988, I was asked down to London to present the 6am to 7am slot at *TV-am* for a week as holiday cover. I'm afraid I was dreadful. Nobody is great when they first start presenting, and you need to get experience under your belt to settle in and improve. I was thrown in headfirst and I hadn't a clue what I was doing. If social media had been around then I would have been totally destroyed. I can just imagine the toxic tweets.

Somehow, I survived the week and got invited back. I improved as time went on and I kept getting asked to stay for another week, and then another one. Before I knew it, I was presenting the main show with the late, great Mike Morris.

I steadied my nerves, took on board every piece of advice I was given and I focused on improving. Whether you work as a teacher or a nurse or you're a West End star, experience is vital. Practice makes perfect (although to be fair, I still don't think I was a very good waitress by the time I quit that particularly tough job!).

IMPOSTER SYNDROME

I think we're still a class-ridden society in the UK. No matter what you do in your career, if you were working class like me, you never really lose that feeling that you aren't quite good enough. I know now that that's daft, but for years my background made me feel insecure and not quite as good as other people.

Even as a child, I worried about school, I fretted about getting top marks, I lost sleep over whether I was clever enough, and I still worry that I'm going to be 'found out' one day. I was so relieved when I found out that this feeling has name: 'imposter syndrome'. It seems to be particularly prevalent in women, but I do wonder if that's just because men don't talk about it as much?

For years, I thought I had my job due to pure luck. Then recently I thought, 'Hang on a minute, I've now been doing this job for 35 years. If I wasn't any good at it I would have been "found out" by now. No one is keeping me on the telly out of the goodness of their heart, or as some sort of charity case.'

My contract gets renewed every couple of years and I'm lucky that it has been taken up time and time again. But let me tell you,

three months before it's up for renewal, I am so anxious. I'm up at three o'clock in the morning panicking about it and thinking of a Plan B in case it all goes belly-up.

Some people find uncertainty perfectly manageable, but not me. I realise that I'm incredibly lucky to do the job I do and I never take it for granted. I think part of my insecurity harks back to when I was working for *GMTV* and was on maternity leave with Rosie.

She was born in June and I was expecting to go back three months later, in September, because you don't get maternity leave when you're freelance. My contract was not renewed and I was basically sacked. I got a call from my boss out of the blue two weeks before I was due to go back on air, saying that I didn't need to come back as they had someone new. They'd employed Anthea Turner in my place and I was out on my ear.

In TV, especially back then, presenters were like baskets of dollies; a new boss might come in and say, 'I don't like that dark-haired dolly. I'm going to give that one to charity and get a new one,' and you're out.

Telly is a tough game, but my sacking felt particularly brutal. I was told not to take it personally, but I couldn't help it and it stung. Steve was working as a freelance cameraman, so neither of us were guaranteed a salary, and when I got that call saying that my contract wasn't being renewed it was a huge blow.

At that point I really didn't mind what I did for work. I didn't care if I ended up in front of the camera or behind it, I just needed to earn money. I didn't care about losing the 'fame' either, because I can take or leave that side of it, but I needed to work to help pay the bills.

With Rosie just a couple of months old, I had to pull on my big girl pants, stick her under one arm and my CV under the other, and go around every TV station with my show reel.

I think some people who interviewed me secretly enjoyed telling someone with so much experience that there was nothing on offer. One executive from BBC Scotland asked if I could speak Gaelic, and when I said sadly I did not, I was told I was no use to them, which was tough to hear. I won't lie, for a time I felt totally out of the loop and wondered if my career was over.

Just months after giving birth, I was carrying a fair amount of pregnancy weight, my boobs were leaking, I had massive bags under my eyes and I couldn't fit into any of my old clothes. I was never going to be one of those celeb mums that elected to have a Caesarean and a tummy tuck at the same time so I could fit back into my jeans in a week, but I was at the other end of the scale and it wasn't doing my confidence any good.

I kept hitting brick walls, but I knew from my experience with 'accent-gate' that you can't fall into despair or it will become much harder to bounce back. If you let doubts and fears eat away at your self-esteem and self-belief, you're done for. So despite my panic, I kept reminding myself that I would be all right. If nothing else I could go back to being a waitress. Albeit a terrible one.

Come October, I was still unemployed. I was waiting to hear back about a few bits and bobs when I got a call from my old employers at *GMTV*. They told me that a baby food manufacturer wanted to sponsor a new 'Mum and Baby' slot, but they would only go ahead if I was the one who presented it. The deal was that I would work every Tuesday and Thursday for half an hour from 9am.

Of course I wanted to tell them where to get off after being so ignominiously given the boot, but I'm not daft. It was a brilliant opportunity and the chance for much-needed work. The campaign ran in November and December and did so well that I was given my very own show in the New Year. Decades later, I'm still here!

When I look back at the experience, I'm proud of my resilience, but while I should have been enjoying spending time with my new baby, instead I was full of anxiety and feeling like a failure. I can never get those months back, but there's no point in being bitter and I just have to chalk it up to experience. What doesn't kill you makes you stronger.

When you start out in any industry you have to put the graft in, but I always try to help other people. There is nothing worse than seeing a boss climbing to the top of the career ladder and wielding all the power and then pulling up that ladder so no one can follow them to the top.

I especially hate it when women bosses feel they have to be ballsier than the men. They don't. We're supposed help others, that's how it works, and shame on you if you don't. So many people helped me along the way and now I want to pay it forward, so I make a conscious effort to give others a leg up, even if it's just when they ask me for advice. We all need support and encouragement, whether we're dipping our toes into new waters or you're at the top of your game.

Here are a few things I've learned about how to tackle imposter syndrome head-on:

- *Realise that no one else has got you to where you are today. You've done it off your own bat. Stop telling yourself you've been lucky, you are where you are because you deserve it.*

- *Remember that the world is not going to fall apart if you make a mistake or don't do something as well as you would like to. Dust yourself off and try again.*

- *Keep in mind that if you feel terrible it will rub off on other people. So really, you're doing everyone a favour by having self-belief.*

- *Don't compare yourself to anyone else, especially not in a work situation. I cannot say this enough times. It's pointless and corrosive.*

- *Keep a note of all the positive things people have said about you and look at it whenever you're doubting yourself.*

- *Remember, it's not just you! Loads of celebrities, including Michelle Pfeiffer, Tom Hanks and Lady Gaga, have admitted to suffering from imposter syndrome. You don't look at them and think they were 'getting away with it'.*

FINDING PURPOSE IN
TOUGH MOMENTS

I have come across some incredibly inspirational people and I'll often get asked, 'Is it amazing meeting Hugh Jackman?' and yes, it is a special day when I get to hang out with him, and yes, he is the loveliest man in all of the world. But the interviews I truly remember are with the so-called 'ordinary' people who have overcome the most horrendous tragedies and somehow managed to move on with their lives.

For instance, I'm consistently amazed at people's capacity to forgive. I interviewed Brian Aim, father of a young girl from Orkney called Karen who was murdered while she was travelling in New Zealand. I asked Brian if he could forgive her murderer and he said he could. I said he was a far better human being than me, and he replied, 'If I don't forgive I'll be eaten up with rage and hate and that would destroy her memory.'

Brian died in 2018, and I will never forget him, or his words of compassion and forgiveness in the face of unimaginable loss.

I think meeting or even hearing about extraordinary people like Brian helps all of us. I know that if I'm down and I meet someone who is going through something really tough it will hit home and pull me out of whatever hole I may find myself in.

I was having a hard time when something untrue was written about me in the press and I was very upset about it. The next day I did a photo shoot with my wonderful producer, Helen Addis, who had been diagnosed with breast cancer, and I thought to myself, 'What am I moaning about? I've got a cheek feeling sorry for myself when our Helen is going through such an ordeal.'

Helen has dealt with her illness with bravery, tenacity and, above all, a wonderful sense of humour. When I found out about her diagnosis I was totally floored. She's only 39, a mum of three and really healthy, so it was a shock.

She's truly inspirational and I'm so proud of her. As horrendous as it's been for her, she has made sure that something incredible has come out of a terrible situation, because we launched our 'Change and Check' campaign through which we've asked shops to put stickers on mirrors in changing rooms to remind women to check their boobs. It was all her idea and has already saved lives.

Breast cancer affects one in eight women and we all need to be vigilant. Reminders are essential because it's one of those things that can easily slip your mind, and it may well save your life.

MY HERO HELEN

I wanted to include an interview with Helen in this book, not only to help inform women about breast cancer, but also because she is a shining example of how you can come out the other side of a horrendous situation with grace and knowledge, and help to make a difference in the world.

Helen, when did you first realise something wasn't right?

I was getting ready for work one morning, and as I put on my body moisturiser my hand ran over my right boob and I noticed a hard lump, about the size of a chickpea. I was 39, fit and well. I don't smoke, I don't drink much, and there's no family history of breast cancer, so I thought it must be hormonal. We had a guest on the show that morning who had stage four bowel cancer and she said, 'If you notice anything different about your body, get it checked out.' I saw that as a sign.

So you saw your doctor right away?

I did, and they agreed it was probably hormonal. I was referred to a consultant and by the time I saw them two weeks later, another four lumps had grown. I had a biopsy and a mammogram, and four days after that I was called in and told it was aggressive breast cancer. Life flipped in that moment. I'm used to working full-time and looking after three small children and, to be honest, I didn't have time for it. I didn't have time for bloody cancer!

How did you feel after you got your diagnosis?

It was really weird. I took the kids to school the next day and I saw all the familiar faces in the playground and I thought, 'They have no idea how much my life has changed.' At that stage I didn't know if it had spread anywhere. My husband and I kept it to ourselves while I had more scans. Luckily the results showed there wasn't an obvious mass anywhere else in my body. But once we knew and we were fully informed, there's the whole question of how you tell people you have cancer.

That must have been so tough.

It was. We told the children first, and then we started telling the rest of our family and friends. When you see other people scared, it scares you too. The kids were kind of ok about it. My youngest daughter was five at the time so I don't think she really understood, but my nine-year-old son was very direct with his questions. He asked me if I had cancer and if it was going to kill me, which was heartbreaking.

Your treatment started almost immediately, didn't it?

I had a mastectomy a week after my diagnosis, and four weeks after that I went into 16 rounds of chemo, followed by 15 rounds of radiotherapy. My cancer is HER2-positive and oestrogen-receptive, meaning there's a protein and a hormone in my body that feeds the cancers. They have to be suppressed so that naughty cells won't be fed. As a result, the doctors artificially started my menopause, so I'm dealing with the hot sweats and the mood swings and everything else that goes with it at the moment.

You've been through such an awful time and I know how incredibly lucky you feel to be coming out the other side.

I feel so grateful I caught my breast cancer when I did. I met another woman who had the same diagnosis as me but she kept putting off going to the doctor. Sadly, she's in palliative care now, but it's so treatable if you catch it early so I'm trying to spread the word. Know your body, and if you notice something different, don't ignore it. As women, especially, we spend so much time looking after everyone around us that we don't always notice when something is wrong with us. People often say that breast cancer gets talked about a lot and that other cancers need to be spoken about too, which I understand. Breast cancer's still the most diagnosed cancer in women, but it's also one of the most treatable.

I remember you telling me that you felt guilty when you got your diagnosis, which seems crazy, but once you explained why, I got it.

I felt so guilty about what my husband went through because I thought, 'He didn't sign up for this.' I felt awful that I was putting him through everything, but it was a natural reaction. I also felt like I'd let my kids down, but all of those things kick-started me into taking control and owning the situation. I was grateful it was me that got the diagnosis and not my husband or my kids, because I don't think I could have handled that. At least I felt like I was more in control because it was happening to me. I lost my mum halfway through chemo as well, and I did then think, 'What have I done to deserve this?' I'm still trying to get my head around it all, but the support I've had has been amazing.

How has your experience changed you?

It's changed me massively. I've learned so much about myself, and I've learned to put myself first a lot more. Not in a selfish way, but now I don't feel guilty if I say I'm not going to do something or go somewhere. It sounds so obvious but I just appreciate life a little bit more. If I go out on a walk now, I really take in what's around me. I didn't really look at trees and nature in general before, but I notice everyday things so much more.

I was very much a future person and always thinking about what I had to do next, rather than living and enjoying the moment.

In a strange way, now I know I'm going to survive it, I wouldn't change my diagnosis for the world. It's flipped everything upside down and I've come out a much stronger, more grounded, calmer person. It's put life into perspective. I'm also a lot more aware of what I'm putting in my body. I was so cheesed off with my body to begin with, because I felt like I'd looked after it and it had let me down, but now I appreciate it so much because it's supported me incredibly.

The way you eat has changed a lot, hasn't it?

I definitely look at the plate in front of me now and think, 'What good am I going to get out of this?' I was brought up on quite processed food, so give me chicken Kiev, chips and beans for dinner and I am as happy as Larry. I still have that once a week because I love it, but I'm a bit more balanced and in tune with my body these days. I eat and drink a lot more healthily than I did before my diagnosis, and I feel different. I feel like I respect myself a lot more. I'm not sure if that's because I've had so many drugs pumped through me and I'm more aware of how quickly you can react to what goes into your body. I crave good stuff, and I'm much more focused on that now.

And you're much better at taking time out for yourself.

It's more important to me than ever, I think it's essential. There's a school of thought that everyone has pre-cancerous cells in their body, and there are questions about what causes them to mutate. I strongly believe that my illness was down to stress. I can almost pinpoint when it happened, and a lot of the women that have had a similar diagnosis to me have said the same. I wasn't looking after my mental state well enough, and I'm much more careful about that now and I make sure I take time out to relax. We try to be stoic and we don't address things, whereas now I know my body so much better than I did before, and I know when it needs a break.

And you've discovered reiki!

I know! I never thought that would be my bag but it's really helped me. The lady I see works with crystals and all sorts, and she's a trained nutritionist, so she's helped me with that side of things too. I didn't think reiki would be for me but I went in with an open mind, and I would recommend anyone to do the same. It's whatever gets you through, really. Even if it's just a case of you relaxing and letting go for an hour, find what works for you.

What has your experience taught you about friendship?

It's taught me just how important good friends are. I have lost touch with friends along the way, which is a shame. I haven't deliberately done that and there haven't been any arguments, but when you go through something like cancer, you realise who your real friends are, and it's been quite surprising to see who has been there and who hasn't. I'm at peace with that and I know that everyone is busy with their own lives but it's put things in perspective.

Of course, the wonderful thing to come out of such a terrible situation is the Check and Change campaign.

If I'm being honest, I can't believe how much it's taken off. It's just a sticker and it's such an obvious thing to do, it should have been done before. The response has been overwhelming, and the amount of people that have contacted us to say they've found something while they've been checking their boobs is unbelievable, and all from a sticker on a mirror! I'm so pleased that something positive has come out of a bad situation, and I think it's helped me get through it in a way. The campaign has been life-changing for some people. It's all about spreading the word and informing people about the symptoms. It was even endorsed by Madonna and Naomi Campbell, and was mentioned in the House of Commons.

Breast cancer signs to look out for:

- *Lumps in breast or armpit*
- *Swelling*
- *Bloody discharge from the nipples*
- *Dimpling on the nipples*
- *Rash on your breasts*
- *Nipple inversion*
- *Unusual pain*
- *Colour change/redness*

Always see your doctor about any changes.

Even if someone has had the worst possible experience, I try to find something uplifting to focus on. Of course, with some people it's just not possible, for instance with Kate and Gerry McCann. The interview I did with them shortly after their daughter Madeleine disappeared is one of the toughest I've ever had to do, but it was so important to them because they needed to keep Madeleine in the public eye.

All of these years later, I still can't even begin to imagine the hell they've been through. They've been so dignified, even when they were horribly attacked and trolled by conspiracy theorists who have accused them of murdering their own child. I have been sickened by the abuse heaped on this couple, who will never have peace of mind until they know what happened to their child.

Covering the horrific Dunblane massacre in 1996, when 16 primary school children and their teacher were killed by a gunman, was particularly distressing. Eamonn Holmes and I did a special edition of *GMTV* live the next day from outside Dunblane Cathedral. We both wept after that show.

What I didn't know was that some of the families were watching, including Pam Ross, whose daughter Joanna was murdered. She asked her police liaison officer to get in touch with me privately as she needed someone to talk to, in confidence and under the radar.

Pam and I just clicked. She had a tiny baby daughter, Alison, at the time and I took along photos of Rosie, who was only two, and we sat and talked for hours. I was honoured to be asked to attend Joanna's funeral and to speak at the memorial service in

Dunblane Cathedral, and as their parents walked up to the altar and lit a candle, I read out the names of every child that had been shot and killed.

Those mothers and fathers went through hell and I have so much admiration for them and for their brave gun control campaign that will have undoubtedly saved lives. Pam is a friend to this day, and one of the bravest women I have ever known.

Some days I speak to people who have been through the worst experiences imaginable. I need to make sure they walk away from talking to me feeling as if they have done themselves proud.

Going on live TV is not easy and sometimes people are crippled with nerves. I need to gain their trust and make them as relaxed as possible, so I always try to sit down with people before I do an interview. It's not to go through questions, because although I have done my research and have the information in my head, I have conversations with my guests. And a list of prepared questions makes for a very stilted interview. What's essential is that they go away feeling like they've said what they need to.

When I recently interviewed Steve Bland, who lost his wife Rachael to breast cancer, I wanted him to know that he'd done justice to his amazing wife and had said all he needed to say. He was inspirational and she would have been so very proud of him. I think it's very important that even when someone is going through the worst possible time they feel that they can find a little bit of light, no matter how small. Steve is helping to raise funds and awareness about cancer, so the interview was very important to him.

If my enthusiasm for my job ever waned I would have to call it quits because it's so important to me that my work is worthwhile. It's all very well slapping on a smile when you're having a bad day, but I have to have a personal connection with the work I do. Not everyone feels that way; some people prefer to do jobs they're not emotionally connected to and find meaning in other parts of their lives.

We all have to put on a brave face if we are going through difficult times. My dad has been very ill recently, he's not out of the woods but he's getting better and stronger every day. Of course, I've been incredibly worried about him, but I have to leave those concerns at the studio door and put on my TV face, as no one wants to see me being teary and upset.

I feel so grateful to still be doing a job that allows me to meet interesting, fascinating, and even occasionally annoying people. I've been inspired, amused and baffled, and every single day is different.

It's perfect for me.

EXERCISE

What would your dream job look like? Instead of thinking of job titles,
list what's most important to you: stability, flexible hours, helping
others? Use that list as your starting point. Sometimes we get so
caught up with ambition or comparing ourselves to others that we
forget to make sure we're genuinely happy with the path we're taking.

The perfect job would be . . .

_____

_____

_____

_____

_____

_____

_____

THE WORLD IS YOURS
TO EXPLORE

If I could give one piece of advice to people of any age it would be: 'be curious'. The world is fascinating and there is so much to discover. Not everyone has the means to travel but you can still experience such a lot. If you can't afford to travel, pop down a TV rabbit hole and let the likes of David Attenborough show you the magic of the world.

Don't ever be tired of life; you've only got one, so live it in the best way you can and squeeze out every single drop of happiness you can. Keep your lust for life for as long as possible.

It's great to have pals of all ages so you can get different perspectives on life. Spending time in older people's company can be hilarious and enlightening. The new generation always think they've discovered everything from sex to spirituality, but the same things have been around forever and older people know a hell of a lot more about the world than we do.

All of us, but particularly younger people, could learn so much by listening to our elders. Not in a patronising way, but with respect and an open mind. Inspiration can come from the strangest places, and you can learn amazing things from having a simple conversation. Time, experience and knowledge are invaluable gifts for your daughters, sons, grandchildren and the world at large.

We need more mentor systems for older people to pass on their knowledge. How wonderful would it be if people of advanced years could pass on their insight and say, 'I've been through that so you don't have to, and here's the best way to deal with it.'

There's a wonderful initiative called the University of the Third Age. If you've retired you can set up a group and talk about absolutely anything, from astronomy to horse racing. My mum loves it. She's learning German at the age of 78 and she's enjoying the company of new people. It's a brilliant scheme where you can make friends and share knowledge, and I hope it becomes more widely available because it's a lifeline for some people, particularly those who are lonely.

Curiosity is what keeps me young. I am curious about *everything*. I went to see Michael Palin give a talk at the Royal Geographical Society and he said that of all the things, of all the human traits that you should retain when you're getting older, it is CURIOSITY. He is a wise man.

I'm interested in the world, and that keeps *me* interesting. I've got such a thirst for knowledge I want to read every book and watch every documentary and movie going. I think it's important not to lose your sense of wonder. Look at little kids when they see something that interests them, they'll stand for ages looking and taking it all in, completely absorbed, and we should all embrace that inquisitive child inside us.

The world is a beautiful place and I want to know everything about it, and the people who live in it. We learn more about ourselves by getting out and experiencing life and finding out what we can achieve and what we can give back.

I find other people much more interesting than I do myself. That's important both for my job and simply because I want to grow as a human being.

DON'T WAIT TO START YOUR BUCKET LIST!

Bucket lists are generally seen as something we do when we get older or retire, but why wait to make a start on yours? Crack on right away and start doing things that will make you proud and uplifted.

Your list doesn't need to be full of things like going to the top of the Empire State Building or doing a parachute jump. It could be learning to swim or doing a charity walk. Put everything on your list and go for it.

EXERCISE

I think you know what's coming . . . Start your bucket list this very minute. Write down everything you would love to do, no matter how crazy. My current list is below. Some of the things on it are a bit bonkers, and some of yours should be too!

- *Go whale watching in Greenland.*

- *Take the Trans-Siberian Express from Moscow to Vladivostok.*

- *Wheel around a barrow load of baby orangutans in Borneo.*

- *Be an extra in the sci-fi series* The Orville.

- *Learn to speak Spanish fluently.*

- *Be a guest backing singer with Human League during one of those fabulous nostalgia concerts.*

- *Get a behind-the-scenes tour of NASA in Houston, Texas.*

- *Walk the West Highland Way.*

- *Be a terrifying baddie in a TV crime thriller.*

My bucket list

_____

_____

_____

_____

_____

_____

_____

_____

_____

_____

_____

BYE FOR NOW!

Thanks so much for reading. I really hope you enjoyed my book and were able to pick up some great tips that will enable you to go out into the world and shine like you deserve to! I'm going to dedicate the final few sentences to my formidable but rather amazing Granny Mac.

When I was young, she used to tell my brother, cousins and me the most fabulous howlers about how she was descended from the Russian royal family and all sorts of other tall tales. Some of her stories were utterly ridiculous, but she also talked a lot of sense. She would always tell us, 'You've got to seize the day.' It's still the best piece of advice I've ever been given.

If anyone bought her perfume as a present she would use up the lot in a week. Even if she was just taking the bins out she would drench herself in scent. She would wear her best clothes even if she was staying in. She didn't ever save anything or hold back 'just in case'. Nothing was kept for 'best'. Even when she got to the age of 82, she only reluctantly went to the local old-aged pensioners' club because, as she put it, it was 'full of aged relics'.

And she *wasn't* old. She was funny, she was feisty, and she absolutely knew that the best way to live your life is the way that makes you happiest.

Come on, let's all be a bit more Granny Mac. Dig out your fancy underwear, spritz on that special perfume and wear your brand-new dress to the supermarket. Let's make *every* day shine!

LOVELY LISTS

If you're looking for some inspiration to keep your 'shine'
journey going, then look no further! Here are some of my
personal favourites.

SONGS

'Shine' – Take That

'Club Tropicana' – Wham!

'Cake by the Ocean' – DNCE

'Happy' – Pharrell Williams

'On the Floor' – JLo, feat. Pitbull

'Give Me the Night' –
George Benson

'All Night Long' – Lionel Richie

'No Scrubs' – TLC

'Get Lucky' – Daft Punk, feat.
Pharrell Williams

'Celebration' – Kool and
the Gang

'Never Too Much' –
Luther Vandross

'Dancing Queen' – ABBA

'Crazy In Love' – Beyoncé

'Uptown Funk' – Mark Ronson,
feat. Bruno Mars

'Walking on Sunshine' – Katrina
and the Waves

'I Gotta Feeling' – Black
Eyed Peas

'Shake It Off'– Taylor Swift

'I'm Gonna Be (500 Miles)' –
The Proclaimers

'Can't Get You Out Of My Head'
– Kylie Minogue

'Fill Me In' – Craig David

'Starman' – David Bowie

'A Girl Like You' – Edwyn Collins

'Labour of Love' – Hue and Cry

'Reasons to be Cheerful, Part 3'
– Ian Dury and the Blockheads

'Rock Your Body' –
Justin Timberlake

'Don't Stop Me Now' – Queen

'I Don't Feel like Dancin'' –
Scissor Sisters

'Hips Don't Lie' – Shakira

'Sunrise' – Simply Red

'Yeah!' – Usher

'September' – Earth, Wind
and Fire

'Just Dance' – Lady Gaga

'Moves Like Jagger' – Maroon 5,
feat. Christina Aguilera

MOVIES

The Adventures of Priscilla,
Queen of the Desert

Some Like It Hot

Singin' in the Rain

It's a Wonderful Life

Dumbo (the original cartoon)

All About Eve

Anything by the Marx Brothers

Deadpool

Love Actually

Sense and Sensibility

Emma

Galaxy Quest

Happy Feet

Mamma Mia

The Full Monty

Forrest Gump

The Birdcage (both French and
US versions)

My Big Fat Greek Wedding

Beauty and the Beast (original
cartoon)

When Harry Met Sally

Toy Story

Despicable Me

The Wizard of Oz

Elf

The Greatest Showman

TV

Poldark (both versions)

Pride and Prejudice

Frasier

Star Trek (original series)

Curb Your Enthusiasm

RuPaul's Drag Race

An Audience With Billy Connolly

The Good Life

Ever Decreasing Circles

Mum

Father Ted

The Great British Bake Off

Queer Eye (Netflix reboot)

Friends

Cheers

Modern Family

The Big Bang Theory

The Durrells in Corfu

Glee

BOOKS

Anything by Maeve Binchy or Marian Keyes

South – Sir Ernest Shackleton

To Kill a Mockingbird – Harper Lee

Tipping the Velvet – Sarah Waters

A Christmas Carol – Charles Dickens

Fried Green Tomatoes at the Whistle Stop Cafe – Fannie Flagg

The Hundred-Year-Old Man Who Climbed out of the Window and Disappeared – Jonas Jonasson

The No. 1 Ladies' Detective Agency – Alexander McCall Smith

Notes from a Small Island – Bill Bryson

Greenvoe – George Mackay Brown

RESOURCES

BACP - British Association for Counselling and Psychotherapy
www.bacp.co.uk

BorrowMyDoggy
www.borrowmydoggy.com

BPS - British Psychological Society
www.bps.org.uk

Bronagh Webster
Instagram - @bronaghwebster
Twitter - @bronaghstylist

Dr Louise Newson
www.newsonhealth.co.uk

HCPC - The Health and Care Professions Council
https://www.hcpc-uk.org

Helen Addis
Instagram - @thetittygritty

Download the Check and Change sticker
https://www.itv.com/lorraine/health/download-the-change-and-check-sticker

Helen Hand
Instagram - @helenhandmakeup
Twitter - @helenhandmakeup

Lorri Craig
www.lorricraig.com

Maxine Jones
www.maxicise.tv

NHS
www.nhs.uk

Refuge
www.refuge.org.uk

Relate
www.relate.org.uk

The Complementary and Natural Healthcare Council
www.cnhc.org.uk

The Samaritans
www.samaritans.org

UKCP - UK Council for Psychotherapy
https://www.psychotherapy.org.uk

Wildlife Trusts
www.wildlifetrusts.org

Womens Aid
www.womensaid.org.uk

ACKNOWLEDGEMENTS

Behind every book is a team of people and so many people helped bring *Shine* to life! Firstly, thank you to my interviewees for generously sharing your wisdom and expertise: Bronagh Webster, Helen Addis, Helen Hand, Lorri Craig, Dr Louise Newson and Maxine Jones. Thank you to everyone at Penguin Random House for their hard work, in particular Susan Sandon, Zennor Compton, Joanna Taylor, Charlotte Bush, Klara Zak, Sarah Ridley, Mat Watterson, Claire Simmonds, Sasha Cox, Laura Garrod, Lauren Nesworthy, Jess Barnfield and Ceara Elliot. Thank you to my agents, Professor Jonathan Shalit OBE, Miranda Chadwick and Jamie Slattery. Finally, thank you to Chloe Hall for the beautiful illustrations and Abi Hartshorne for the gorgeous design. Every single one of you put a little bit of light into the publication of this book and I couldn't be more grateful.

1 3 5 7 9 10 8 6 4 2

Century
20 Vauxhall Bridge Road
London SW1V 2SA

Century is part of the Penguin Random House group of companies
whose addresses can be found at global.penguinrandomhouse.com.

Copyright © Lorraine Kelly 2019
Photos on pages 9, 10, 18, 56, 79, 83, 125, 148,
163, 199, 223, 227, 241: courtesy of the author
Photo on page 161: Getty/Karwai Tang
Photo on page 176: Steve Meddle/Shutterstock

Lorraine Kelly has asserted her right to be identified as the author of this
Work in accordance with the Copyright, Designs and Patents Act 1988.

First published in Great Britain by Century in 2019

www.penguin.co.uk

A CIP catalogue record for this book is available from the British Library.

ISBN 9781529124477

Printed and bound in Germany by APPL aprinta druck, Wemding

Penguin Random House is committed to a sustainable future for our
business, our readers and our planet. This book is made from
Forest Stewardship Council® certified paper.